DARLENE GAIL WELLS

Letting God Reign

Experiencing God and His Transforming Power

First published by Darlene Gail Wells 2020

Copyright © 2020 by Darlene Gail Wells

All rights reserved. No part of this publication may be reproduced, stored or transmitted in any form or by any means, electronic, mechanical, photocopying, recording, scanning, or otherwise without written permission from the publisher. It is illegal to copy this book, post it to a website, or distribute it by any other means without permission.

Darlene Gail Wells has no responsibility for the persistence or accuracy of URLs for external or third-party Internet Websites referred to in this publication and does not guarantee that any content on such Websites is, or will remain, accurate or appropriate.

Designations used by companies to distinguish their products are often claimed as trademarks. All brand names and product names used in this book and on its cover are trade names, service marks, trademarks and registered trademarks of their respective owners. The publishers and the book are not associated with any product or vendor mentioned in this book. None of the companies referenced within the book have endorsed the book.

All Scripture quoted is from the King James Version of the Bible, unless otherwise noted.

First edition

ISBN: 978-1-7356944-0-5

This book was professionally typeset on Reedsy. Find out more at reedsy.com

To my husband Dale - you are my gift from God and the love of my life. Thank you for the way you show me the love of Christ, every single day. I love you forever and always.

The Lord is my strength and my shield; my heart trusted in him, and I am helped: therefore my heart greatly rejoiceth; and with my song will I praise him.

Psalm 28:7

Contents

Acknowledgement   iii

I   Letting God Reign

Chapter 1 - Surrendering it All	3
Chapter 2 - A Love Story From God	9
Chapter 3 - Purposefully Alive in Christ	26
Chapter 4 - In Unity and Forgiveness We Thrive	34
Chapter 5 - The Many Ways He Speaks	39
Chapter 6 - Becoming a Prayer Warrior	45
Chapter 7 - Shining Like a Diamond	48
Chapter 8 - He Hears Me!	52
Chapter 9 - Tossing Mountains Into the Sea	57
Chapter 10 - A Dreamer Dreaming Dreams	60
Chapter 11 - Saved For a Purpose	65
Chapter 12 - Let God Be God	68
Chapter 13 - Devotion Takes Courage	72
Chapter 14 - A Shoebox Full of Love	75
Chapter 15 - Jesus Wept	78
Chapter 16 - A Door Closes, But Another Opens	80
Chapter 17 - Giving it All to God	86
Chapter 18 - Let Your Light Shine!	89
Chapter 19 - A Gently Beckoning Voice	92
Chapter 20 - Peace in His Presence	95
Chapter 21 - Finding My War Room	99

Chapter 22 - Exhibiting Holiness	104
Chapter 23 - Sharing the Gift of Jesus	106
Chapter 24 - Courage, Dear Heart	109
Chapter 25 - All for King Jesus	112
Chapter 26 - Seeing the Good in the Struggle	118
About the Author	125

Acknowledgement

First and foremost, I would like to thank my wonderful husband Dale for being behind me one hundred percent when the Lord called me to write this book. I would not have been able to do this without your love, support and encouragement. You are my gift from God and I love you more than words can ever express. Thank you for the joy you have brought into my life and for making me smile and laugh continually! Most of all, I thank you for showing me the love of Christ, every single day. You are my favorite person, and will be forever and always.

I would also like give thanks to our Senior Pastor, Dr. Harold Phillips and Associate Pastor, Dr. Joshua Phillips of Pleasant View Baptist Church in Port Deposit, Maryland. I thank you both for your truth-filled, inspiring teaching of God's Word which has influenced me greatly and helped me to grow spiritually throughout my journey as a born again believer. I am so blessed to be a part of your church family.

I would also like to thank my daughter Ashley Heyn for always being my sidekick, my best friend, someone who can always make me laugh no matter what. When I gave birth to you, I had no idea that you would end up being my BFF and we would have so many crazy adventures together! Thank you for telling me about Jesus and for not giving up when I rejected what you were telling me. Your persistence paid off and I am eternally grateful. You are an amazing woman and such a joy to my life. Also a joy to me is my loving and incredibly talented son Trevor Eilers. I am so proud of your drive and determination to succeed, and to do what is necessary to achieve that success. I am also so very proud of your musical talent, and I absolutely love to hear you playing that piano. You are amazing.

To my stepsons Christopher and Jesse Wells, their wives Katie and Sarah, and my son-in-law Daniel Heyn: I thank you all from the bottom of my heart for accepting me into your family and showing me what a loving Christ-centered family is all about. I love you all and I thank the Lord for placing each and every one of you in my life.

I want to praise and thank the Lord for blessing Dale and I with five wonderful grandchildren; Sophia, Emma, Elijah, Micah and Emma. You light up my world with joy and love, and I adore seeing life through your precious little eyes.

I would like to give special thanks to my family; My parents Robert and Jane Michiels, my brother Bobby Michiels, and sisters Jill Michiels and Gail Coyne. Thank you for loving me and always being there for me. Thank you Mom for all of your prayers, and for always cheering me on and giving me encouragement. Thank you Dad for your love and for all the fun memories fishing and boating when we were kids. (Even that one when we were out in the ocean in that little boat and I thought we were all going to die!) I can laugh and smile about that now because it was one of the many happy memories I have of our family time together. To my siblings, you are all amazing people and I am so blessed to call you my family. Thank you for the special memories. I love you all so much!

I

Letting God Reign

Experiencing God and His Transforming Power

Chapter 1 - Surrendering it All

I love to hear stories of how God is working in people's lives. It gives me so much joy because those stories of the Lord showing up and doing amazing things are testimonies of His goodness and His awesome power. It is so exciting when God gets involved because it gives us a little glimpse of who He is and what He can do. When the Lord told me to write a book, I had no idea what kind of book it would be. I listened very carefully to the leading of the Holy Spirit, because I wanted this book to be what He wanted it to be, not what I thought it should be. When I sat down and started writing, the Lord kept reminding me of testimonies of how He has worked in my life. This makes perfect sense to me now because I had been telling God for a long time that if He would keep giving me these testimonies, I would keep sharing them. I had no idea that they would end up being in a book, though.

I have some of my personal testimonies to share with you and what I have learned from them. But first, I'd like to share a little about myself and a few observations and discoveries that I have made along the way.

I have been a broken person. I have lived and loved and lost. I have been stuck in such a dark place that I no longer wanted to live. But then I found Jesus, and that changed everything! He turned my ashes into beauty and my mourning into joy. God's love and mercy shine brightest in our broken places. What we may see as brokenness inside us, God sees as beauty. He sees exactly how He can take that brokenness and build it up into something amazing and beautiful and use it for His glory. But we must be willing to hand it over to Him and let Him do what He needs to do to achieve His good and perfect will for us. Be assured that no matter what your brokenness is - whether it comes from depression, addiction, illness, abuse, grief, or something other than what I have mentioned here, our great and mighty God can heal you and use it to help draw you closer to Him and grow spiritually. God can take whatever it is you are going through and He can turn it into something good. You are His beautiful creation and He loves you more than you can ever imagine. The Bible says that He takes delight in His people and sings over them with joy! He loves when we come to him in our despair and dark places so that He can shine His glorious light in us. The transformation may be difficult and painful at times, but the key is to have the faith of a little child who knows that their Daddy loves them and will always take care of them.

" The Lord thy God in the midst of thee is mighty; he will save, he will rejoice over thee with joy; he will rest in his love, he will joy over thee with singing." ~Zephaniah 3:17

Surrendering yourself to the Lord is the first step. If you are not a Christ follower, I want you to know that Jesus died on the cross to pay the penalty for our sins. We are all sinners and deserve the penalty of death and Hell, but because of God's

CHAPTER 1 - SURRENDERING IT ALL

great mercy and grace, He gave his only Son to die on the cross to pay our sin debt. But Jesus didn't just die. Three days later He arose from the grave and defeated death and Hell! Through our faith in Jesus and what He did on the cross, we are forgiven of our sins and our souls are assured of eternity in Heaven when our mortal bodies die. It also opens the door for us to have a relationship with our Creator. From the moment that we accept Jesus Christ as our Lord and Savior and submit ourselves to Him, He will begin to slowly start working on us. He starts to mold us to become more like Him. This can only take place if we submit ourselves to His lordship over us.

I would like to tell you about how I came to know Jesus. I was a very unhappy individual and I struggled with depression for many years. Antidepressant medications did not help me at all, because I believe that my depression was not caused by a chemical imbalance in the brain that many people suffer from. It was due to a very unhappy, unfulfilled life. There was no peace within me. I felt that I had no worth. I was at the point where I was hearing the words, "I want to die" over and over in my head all day long, and the only reason that I did not end it all was because of my two children. I just could not do that to them and leave them motherless. I really believe that it was Satan's work, and he was trying to get me to take my own life. But God stepped in.

My daughter Ashley, who was a teenager at the time, met a young man who told her about Jesus. She became a born-again believer, gave her heart to Jesus and was baptized. She started going to church and got very involved in many things there, including the choir. She kept inviting me to church but

I really had no interest in going. I attended church growing up, but the only thing that I recall being taught was to be a good person, help your neighbor, confess your sins, recite a bunch of repetitive prayers and you will be forgiven. I never understood why Jesus died on the cross. When I became an adult and moved away, I just stopped going to church.

Ashley kept trying to tell me about Jesus, but I did not believe what she was telling me. I had never been taught any of the things that she was saying to me. She invited me to the Easter program she was participating in at church and she also asked me to sew a costume for her. That was quite a task, hand-sewing a costume, as I did not have a sewing machine at the time and I am not very skilled at this type of thing. I decided to go to watch her perform in that play, and something very unexpected happened. That evening while watching that Easter drama, the Holy Spirit was really speaking to my heart and I felt as though the Lord was calling me. I can't really explain that intense calling that I felt, but I just knew without a doubt that I needed Jesus. That play helped me to understand the sacrifice that Jesus made on the cross for me. Jesus asked me to be His forever and I said yes! I went to the altar during the invitation time and I gave my heart and my life to Jesus that night. Amazingly, from that moment on, my sadness and depressed feelings were lifted. I never again heard that voice in my head tell me over and over that I wanted to die. I now have a joy that I can't even begin to explain, because my worth and my hope is in Jesus. Jesus died for me, to save me from death and Hell. I am assured that I will go to Heaven when I die. I am no longer separated from God because of my sin, and I have a close and personal relationship with Him now. There is so much joy and peace in that knowledge.

Once you've given your heart completely to the Lord, give Him all your broken pieces and watch what He will do with them! He will put them together in a more beautiful way than you ever thought possible. Prayer is so important because it helps you to develop a close relationship with the Lord. It is not possible to have a relationship with God without prayer. It is how we communicate with our Father in Heaven. Pray without ceasing because God wants to hear our petitions and requests and answer them. He wants to be actively involved in every part of our lives. Prayer also has a way of aligning us with what His will is. When going through a difficult situation, I have found that instead of praying, "Lord, how am I going to do this?", a better prayer is, "Lord, I can't wait to see how YOU do this!" I believe that this gives you hope and shows you have faith in what God is going to do. Then hand the situation over to the Lord and wait expectantly for Him to work, having that child-like faith and knowing that he can do all things. There is absolutely nothing too difficult for the Lord Almighty. He created the heavens and the earth and He created you!

We must remember, however, that how we expect God to work on our situation will not always be how He actually will. His wisdom transcends ours. I am always amazed when I get through something and look back and see what He did and how it transformed me in the process. Surrender it all first, then have faith and wait on the Lord to work on your behalf. Waiting for God is probably the hardest part, but His timing is always perfect. Our transformation is what He is working on when we are going through troubled waters. He is working on our character and our response to difficult situations. Keep your eyes on Jesus and not the trouble you are experiencing. He is worthy of our trust.

Chapter 2 - A Love Story From God

I would now like to tell you about how the Lord has changed my ashes into beauty. In November of 2013, my husband of 27 years announced that he wanted a divorce. It happened one evening just after I arrived home from work. On the drive home that evening, I witnessed the most amazingly breathtaking sunset. It had me so awestruck that I had to stop on the side of the road and take some photos. It really took my breath away and I felt God speaking to me through that beautiful sky. I felt as though He was showing me His glory and that He was telling me how much He loves me and that He was always with me. I absolutely remember thinking those things at the time. It was as if He was comforting me before the storm.

I had no idea that when I arrived at home, my whole world would be shattered. My husband and I had been together since I was about 16 years old and I had never been alone. My life as I knew it would never be the same. He told me that he wanted to see other women and wanted a divorce. I was absolutely devastated. I soon moved out of the home that I so dearly loved and moved into a 3 bedroom apartment with my 21 year old son Trevor and 23 year old daughter Ashley, along with my son-in-law Daniel and newborn granddaughter Sophia. It was Christmas Eve when we all moved into that apartment. Ashley somehow managed to get all of their stuff unpacked, and she also got the Christmas tree and decorations put up by that evening. I was quite amazed and surprised that she was able to accomplish all of that, especially with a newborn infant daughter to care for. I was so thankful that she was able to do it and put a little Christmas joy into an otherwise dismal, depressing time. My heart was filled with so much sadness that day because it was the end of my marriage and the end of our family unit, but it was a new beginning. It was crazy and chaotic at times with 4 adults and a newborn baby in that apartment, but it was filled with love. For the first time, I felt an amazing peace just wash over me and envelop my whole being. I had no more of the stress and anxiety from the situation which I was previously living in. I began to see that God, in His infinite wisdom and mercy, had removed me from there for my own good and well-being.

During this time, I grew intimately close to the Lord. I spent a lot of alone time with Him at a local park, on the fishing pier. It was a special place where I felt that God met with me. I went there practically every day and just prayed and talked with Him, rejoicing in His presence. Some really wonderful things have happened in that place. It never ceases to amaze and excite me when God interacts with me. I would like to tell you about some of the ways that He has done this so that you can get an idea of what I mean.

The first encounter that comes to my mind is the time when I had been watching some bufflehead ducks out on the water. I had only seen them in the distance several times at that point.

CHAPTER 2 - A LOVE STORY FROM GOD

I could see that they were quite fancy looking but I could not get a good look at them since they were so far away. They are a beautiful black and white duck with an iridescent green and purple head. They had never come near the shore while I was there. One day I said, "Lord, I would really love to see those beautiful ducks up close!" Just as the words came out of my mouth, they turned and headed straight for me! They swam right next to the pier and I got to see them up close, just as I had prayed for. The joy spilling out of my heart that day was immense. He showed me that He really does care about everything, big and small. If it is something that we care about, God cares about it too. It seems as though He loves to make us happy with wonderful little surprises such as this.

Another occasion that comes to mind is the day that I arrived at the pier early in the morning. I was full of joyful expectation for that precious time alone with God. As I was standing there at the end of the pier taking in the Lord's beautiful creation and getting ready to pray, I got quite a surprise. All at once, a fish jumped out of the water, a butterfly fluttered by and a bald eagle flew right over me. I was quite astonished when all three of those things happened at the exact same time. That was the most amazing "good morning" I have ever received! I felt so blessed and loved by that unique and wonderful salutation from the Lord.

On another day, I was praying for a friend that was going through an extremely difficult time. When I got done praying, I looked down and there was a cross made of sticks lying on the ground in front of me. I felt very strongly at that moment that the Lord was telling me that He heard my prayers. What a wonderful feeling it is to realize that the Lord God Almighty, the maker of Heaven and Earth, is listening to you. I snapped a photo of the cross with my phone because I was just so amazed by it. On another occasion, I was walking around the park, listening to music through my earbuds. The song I was listening to made reference to Jesus taking the nails (being nailed to the cross) for us. At the exact moment that I heard those lyrics, I looked down and there was a nail lying on the ground! I really felt as though Jesus was reminding me of His sacrifice on the cross. It really made that song come alive for me, and I think about that nail I saw every time I hear it now. One other day, I was sitting in the sunshine at the park gazing out at the beautiful, sparkling water and I started singing a worship song. As I was singing, a bird landed about 6 feet from me and started singing with me! That just absolutely made my day. I have also experienced countless breathtaking sunsets standing on the fishing pier communing with our Creator. You can see by these examples how God can get our attention and bless us in different ways every day. We just have to pay attention.

What beautiful memories I have of spending that time with Jesus in our meeting place. If you don't have a special place where you go to commune with the Lord, I highly recommend that you find one. It can be an indoor or outdoor place, whichever you prefer. I personally prefer the outdoors because you just see so much of God out in His creation. It really helps to draw you closer to Him in all His infinite beauty. I don't currently live close to that park with the fishing pier anymore. I live on a pretty secluded wooded lot, and I often just stand out on the rear deck overlooking the woodlands and talk to the Lord. There were a few times when I was standing out there praying and baby squirrels would come right up to me on the deck and look up at me with their sweet little eyes. It was just absolutely adorable! I have taken some really cute photos of those baby squirrels when they came to visit. Things like that just make the time with the Lord so much sweeter. I feel that He is showing me Himself through nature. I have noticed that those types of things seem to occur when I least expect it, though. I truly believe that God takes delight in surprising us with these little blessings.

If you are fortunate enough to have never experienced divorce, you are blessed. Do whatever you can to avoid it (unless you are in a dangerous or abusive situation), because it is such a heart-wrenching, devastating thing to go through. I can truly understand now why God hates divorce. It was the most difficult thing I have ever experienced, and even though I knew in my heart that God was with me every single moment, I felt so lonely. To me, it was like experiencing the death of a loved one, very much like experiencing grief. I cried so many tears and prayed countless prayers, but I believe that the thing that helped me the most during that time was worship. I worshiped the Lord with all my heart and sang songs of love and praise to the Most High. I have discovered that singing praises to the Lord not only helps you to connect spiritually with Him, but it also reminds you of who He is and how great He is. Knowing that God is in control and is working on our situation really creates a sense of peace.

"Cast thy burden upon the Lord, and he shall sustain thee: he shall never suffer the righteous to be moved." ~Psalms 55:22

You can give it all to the Lord and just rest in Him. He promises to sustain you. Worship Him in the midst of the storm, even if you don't feel like it. You will soon come to treasure that time of connecting.

My relationship with the Lord grew tremendously during that first year on my own. I needed that time to grow in my faith and know that my hope was in Him alone. I also realized that if I was to ever be in another relationship, he would absolutely have to be a Christian man with a love for Jesus that was as deep as mine. Unequally yoked relationships do not usually work out well, as I found out first hand. I decided that I wanted to let God choose my next spouse. I had absolutely no interest in dating around and getting hurt. I had experienced enough hurt and heartache in my life. I prayed fervently for the Lord to send the right man, if it was His will for me to marry again. I asked Him not to let anyone near me unless it was the one that He was sending. I also told Him that I would wait patiently for Him to send the right one, and that He would have to send him right to my doorstep because I was not even going to look. And so I waited, just as I had promised. As I waited, my relationship with the Lord continued to grow and deepen, as did my faith and trust in Him.

A few months later, my trusty little red 1998 Honda (which amazingly had almost 300,000 miles on it), broke down. It died as I was crossing a busy highway, so I was blocking both lanes. It was dark out and it really was a miracle that I wasn't hit by an oncoming vehicle. I had to have it towed home. My son Trevor and I did our best to try to fix it, but we didn't have the proper mechanic's tools to work with. I had my little household tool kit

CHAPTER 2 - A LOVE STORY FROM GOD

which was fine for working around the house, but definitely not for this type of situation. Trevor's tools had been lost somehow when we moved. We spent a couple of weeks trying to fix it to no avail. Being newly single and having to pay rent for an apartment in addition to paying half the mortgage on the house until it sold, I did not have any money to take it to an auto shop to get it fixed. I didn't know what I was going to do, but I trusted that God knew what He was going to do. I was a remote Customer Service Representative at the time and I was working from home most days, so that was a huge blessing. My challenge was to get to the store to go grocery shopping, but more importantly, to get to church. I really felt that I needed my church and my church family to get me through this time in my life. My daughter Ashley and her husband Dan dropped me off at church one day and then came and picked me up after the service at their church was over. Before I left I was speaking with Dr. Harold Phillips, our Senior Pastor at Pleasant View Baptist Church, and I mentioned to him my vehicle issues. He said that he would ask his friend Dale, who is a mechanic, to call me and see if he would come and look at my car. The next day Dale did call me, although he had some difficulty getting through at first because the area code for the phone number he was given for me was incorrect. He succeeded in obtaining the correct number and was able to finally contact me. During our telephone conversation, we discovered that we both attended the same church, but interestingly enough we had never crossed paths before. I told him that I was "the lady with the long blonde hair that sits up in the front of the sanctuary" and he told me that he assisted in back in the sound booth. Neither of us had recalled seeing the other before. So I gave him directions to my place and he came at the appointed time.

The first time I met Dale, it was on a cold December day. He came to my apartment complex and began working on my car. I honestly did not know if I was expected to stand there and wait for him to finish what he was doing or not. I did not want to be rude and just walk away and go inside, so I stayed and stood there awkwardly watching him. I later found out that he was wondering why I was standing there the whole time! I am glad that I did stay, because I learned a lot about him that day. I found out that sadly, he had lost his beloved wife Kathy to Multiple Sclerosis about two and a half years beforehand. She had struggled with it for several years until she passed on to glory. She was a beautiful soul that was well-loved by all and she had a beautiful singing voice. She used her gifts to serve the Lord well. He said that he also had some health struggles of his own for awhile and ended up in the hospital, but he was doing much better. I also found out that day that we are both from Long Island, New York and had both moved to Maryland with our families.

While Dale was working on my car, he happened to look down into the engine compartment and found a tiny spring which had fallen out of the distributor that my son had replaced. It really was a miracle that he found that little spring. That spring was the reason the car wouldn't start, and if it hadn't fallen out of its proper place, I would never have met Dale at that time. I am a firm believer that everything happens for a reason. I was so happy when the car was finally operable again! The very next day, I came out to my car and it had a flat tire. I called roadside assistance to come out and put on the spare tire for me. The gentleman that came out to help me accidentally broke the key for the locking lug nuts on the wheel, so he was unable to put the spare tire on. Once again, I was without a car for a couple of weeks because I had no money to get it fixed. I mentioned the tire problem to Pastor Phillips because he asked me about the car, and he called Dale and asked him if he could assist me again. I had to have my car towed over to the repair shop where he works so he could remove the locking lug nuts from the wheel and then he plugged the tire for me. I went and picked up my car that night and I was so happy to have my car working again.

The next day, as I was driving the car home from the park, my car started overheating. It started snowing and I had to pull over on the shoulder of the highway. The steam was billowing out of the engine compartment. My heart sank. I just could not believe that this was happening. Every time the car was repaired, it broke down the next day again. I got out my cell phone and summoned roadside assistance again to come and tow it home. As I sat there awaiting the tow truck, two young men stopped and offered to fix the car for me. One of them told me that "something told them to stop and help me". They had a young child in their car with them and it was snowing very hard at that point. They told me that they were both diesel mechanics and very graciously began working on the car. After about 30 minutes on the snowy roadside, they had repaired the hose that had the issue and I was on my way. I was so grateful to them for stopping to help me, and to God for sending them. Dale came to my apartment again and replaced the hose. He told me that the rest of the hoses were probably going to go soon. He was correct.

One day soon after that occurred, I picked up a friend to

go to Wednesday evening service at church. Just as we left her apartment and got to a traffic light and stopped, my car started overheating again. I quickly pulled off the road into a parking lot. After opening the hood and doing a brief inspection, I discovered that another one of the hoses was cracked and leaking. My friend decided to run across the road to a convenience store and purchase a roll of duct tape so I could tape up the hose. We were hoping to at least make it to the church parking lot a few miles down the road. As I was working on my taping job, a police officer stopped to see if we were okay. We explained what had happened, and so once I was done with my repairs, he followed behind us to make sure we were not going to break down again. We unfortunately did not make it very far before I saw him turn his lights on so we would pull over because the car was steaming again. We pulled over into another parking lot and attempted to tape up the hose again. When that was accomplished, we went on our way again. Once again, the repair did not hold and the car was steaming again. We were only about a mile and a half from church so we decided to just keep going until we arrived at our destination. The whole way there, we were singing the words, "There is Power in the Name of Jesus". Remembering that our all-powerful Lord was in control of everything really helped to calm me in the middle of this unfortunate and stressful situation.

We finally pulled into the church parking lot with large amounts of steam pouring from my car's engine compartment. It was quite a sight! As soon as we arrived, we jumped out of the car and ran for the church, because at that point we were late. We were so grateful to have gotten there safely. I called my son Trevor to come and pick us up after the service was over and then I asked our Associate Pastor, Pastor Josh, if I could leave the car in the parking lot for a couple of days until I could get it repaired. He said that it would be fine, so I locked it up and left it there.

That evening I posted on social media about my adventures with the steaming Honda. The next thing I knew, Dale contacted me. He had seen what I had posted and happened to be off work the next day, so he told me that he would stop by my apartment and pick up the car key and go over to the church to repair the car. I was so very grateful for his willingness to help me. He was so kind and generous to give of his time once again. At this point, I was really starting to feel that the Lord was whispering to me that Dale was the one that He was sending to me. It truly seemed as though He was pointing to Dale saying, "He is the one!" As I shared earlier, I had prayed that He would not let anyone near me unless he was the right one and I also asked Him to send him "to my doorstep." I could not ignore the fact that Dale had been to my doorstep several times already. I prayed fervently and asked God for a confirmation. I asked that He would open the door for me if Dale was truly the one that He was sending. I also asked that if Dale was not the one, that He would shut the door so that I would know. I was truly shocked when God answered my prayer right away. Immediately after I prayed, I was reading something which contained a scripture verse which jumped out at me and answered my question. It was from Revelation 3:8 and it said, "Behold, I have set before thee an open door, and no man can shut it." When I saw that, I just sat there in utter amazement. I truly felt as though the Lord was speaking to me through that verse. The Lord confirmed to me that day that He had indeed been hearing my prayers and

He answered me in grand fashion, through scripture.

My beloved little red Honda continued to have issues and Dale continued to repair it. Sometimes I would text him questions about the car so I could talk to him. I was always telling him about all the crazy things that were going on with it and we joked about me writing a book called, "The Adventures of Darlene and the Little Red Honda." That car had a special place in my heart. It had been well-loved and well-used for 300,000 miles. My daughter also logged many miles driving that car when she was a teenager. I started calling it my "faith car" because it was very old and was starting to have so many problems that I had to pray and have faith every time that I drove it!

In addition to my occasional texting, sometimes I would stop to talk to Dale at the sound booth on the way out of church on Sunday. That went on for a couple of months, and then one Sunday I was planning on stopping to say hello to him on my way out of church. As I got over by the sound booth, I noticed that he was talking to someone else. I didn't want to be rude and awkward and just stand there, so I proceeded to just keep walking out to the car. When I got into the car, I got this overwhelming feeling that I needed to go back into that church and talk to him. That feeling was very intense and it wouldn't go away. I am absolutely convinced that it was the urging of the Holy Spirit. It was exactly the same type of calling from the Holy Spirit that I experienced on that evening when I walked down the aisle to pray at the altar to be saved and give my heart to Jesus. There was no ignoring it, so I walked back toward the church. Just as I got to the doors, Dale walked out. I greeted him and we started discussing something new going on with my car. He walked me back to the car and offered to take a quick look at it. When he was done inspecting whatever the issue was, we stood there and talked for awhile. Then he unexpectedly asked me if I wanted to go and get some lunch with him. I had been praying for something like this to happen so I gratefully and very excitedly accepted. We picked a place somewhat nearby and agreed to meet there. It was a hot summer day and the air conditioning in my car was not operating. In addition to that, my driver's side window did not roll down. When I arrived at the restaurant, I was a hot and sweaty mess, so I ran into the restroom immediately to try and freshen up a little before he saw me.

We eventually found each other, were seated at our table, and ordered our food. While we waited, we began to talk. I am a very quiet, introverted individual and for me to have a conversation with someone I don't know very well is very difficult. Surprisingly, I did not have that issue conversing with Dale though. What I remember most about that lunch was that we talked and joked the whole time as if we had known each other forever. We spoke about our lives and our families, and our heartaches and joys. We sat and talked for quite some time after finishing our lunch and then we said our goodbyes and went our separate ways. A couple of days later, I sent a text and asked him if he was interested in having dinner with me on Friday or Saturday evening. I had never asked a man out on a date before, but I was getting that urging of the Holy Spirit again. I then saw a quote from Thomas Jefferson that stated, "If you want something you have never had, you must be willing to do something you have never done." So I took the plunge, and sent the invite. After I sent it, I waited for what felt like an eternity, but he did answer me back the following day and accepted the invitation. I was somewhat distressed that it seemed to take so long for him to respond. I later found out that he was having a dialog with God about me. He described it as almost like a "vision" of speaking to God. I knew exactly what he meant when he described it, because I have experienced that as well. The Lord encouraged him regarding me, so he made the decision to go out on the date to see how things went. He had reservations about dating me because apparently I look younger than I actually am and he didn't feel right about dating a younger woman. He mentioned my age on our date, and I advised him of how old I really was and jokingly offered to show him my driver's license to verify it. Once we got that out of the way, I think he felt much better about everything.

After our lovely dinner at a local restaurant, we drove over to the park with the fishing pier and walked around for a while. It was a beautiful summer evening in June, and it was exciting to show him the wonderful place where I spent a lot of my time when I wasn't working. He then drove me home, but neither of us were ready for the evening to end so he suggested that we go out for some ice cream. I gratefully accepted, knowing that would give us a little more time to spend together that evening. After our dessert, we ended up back in my apartment complex parking lot where we sat and talked for a little while. He told me that he had a great time and that he really liked me. He said that he wanted to "take things slow" and get to know me and see what happened. What a wonderful evening it was! Finally, after several months of waiting, things were starting to happen. God is so good and I thanked Him over and over again for all

CHAPTER 2 - A LOVE STORY FROM GOD

He was doing.

Even though Dale had said that he wanted to take things slow, things went very quickly after that initial date. Soon we were seeing each other every evening after work and he was picking me up and taking me to church on Sundays. Four months later on a beautiful October day, we were hiking in the woods in Susquehanna State Park in Maryland. We were enjoying our hike among the Lord's beautiful creation and we stopped to take some photos together. I looked down and started to scroll through the photos to see how they came out, and when I turned around, he was down on one knee with a ring and he asked me to marry him! I was so filled with joy that the tears just flowed from my eyes and I threw my arms around him and answered, "Of course I will!" I couldn't wait to tell everyone about the miracle that God had done in answering my prayers. I asked Him to send the right one and not let anyone else near me, and He did just that! I asked Him to send someone who loves Jesus and to send him right to my doorstep, and that is exactly what He did! There were a few other very specific things that I had prayed for in my future spouse and God gave me every one of them in Dale. I am so thankful and so very blessed. It really is awesome that you can see God's hand in every part of our story. The Lord is so good! What I have learned from this is that if you leave the choice to God, He will always give you His best.

I married Dale, the love of my life, 3 months later. It was a beautiful wedding ceremony held at our church and officiated by our pastor, Dr. Harold Phillips. We were blessed with an unusually warm January day, which was perfect for taking photos outdoors. My daughter Ashley served as my maid of honor and a dear friend was my bridesmaid. They both looked so breathtakingly beautiful in their burgundy red bridesmaid dresses. My son Trevor, who is quite a talented pianist, played the piano beautifully for the ceremony. He played a wedding song that he had written himself and it was absolutely perfect. Dale's older son Christopher was his best man, and his younger son Jesse was his groomsman. Jesse and his family flew in all the way from China, where he was teaching at the time, to be at the wedding. What a joy it was to have all of our children present! Almost all of our family and friends came from out of state to witness our nuptials.

Everything was nearly perfect, however there ended up being a mixup with the delivery of the food for the reception. It was mistakenly delivered to our church's old address. Thankfully, our Pastor's lovely wife Corkie went over to the old church to retrieve it and bring it to the correct location. This delayed the start time of our wedding ceremony, but it was a blessing in disguise because my sister Gail and her family were delayed in their arrival. She and her husband and twin sons drove down from Long Island to Maryland, and if the missing food had not caused a delay, they would have missed the ceremony. They came through the front doors of the church just before I was about to walk down the aisle. I was so happy that they did not miss it! Dale and I are quite sure that the Lord purposefully used the mishap with the food to delay the ceremony. We are so thankful that He did. What initially seemed like a bad situation, all worked out for good. God's timing is always perfect. So the next time you are delayed in something, remember that it may very well be God working something out for good.

CHAPTER 2 - A LOVE STORY FROM GOD

At our wedding ceremony, we braided together a cord of three strands. It symbolizes the unity of the groom, the bride and Jesus. Ecclesiastes 4:12 says, "A cord of three strands is not quickly broken." We are strengthened when Jesus is at the center of our relationships. Something else to remember and hold tightly to is that when you have a conflict with your spouse, you are both on the same team. It should be the two of you against the problem, not the two of you against each other. When you pray together about the problem, it then becomes the three of you against the problem (you, your spouse and Jesus). We have decided that Jesus will always be at the center of our lives and our marriage. Having Him at the center of it all is the best, and only way to have a relationship that is not self-centered and self-serving. Marriage should not just be about what you can get out of it and how your spouse can make you happy. It should be about how you can work together as a team serving the Lord and each other. Pray together, read scripture together and worship together. It really does draw you closer to God and closer to each other.

Chapter 3 - Purposefully Alive in Christ

God has a purpose for each and every one of His children. Some have been called into the ministry as pastors, and some have been called to be missionaries, Sunday school teachers, deacons, worship leaders, etc. Perhaps your role in His kingdom is something more behind-the-scenes. For example, raising children and teaching them about Jesus is a very important one. Every role is equally important to the Lord. 1 Corinthians 12 reminds us that we are many members of one body. Each member has their own part to play, but we need each other. We all need to be collectively working together to become the whole body of Christ and work for the common goal of spreading the gospel and loving the people that God made. Have you discovered what your role is, or do you feel lost and as if you don't know where you are going? I felt as if I was lost in the wilderness for quite some time. I was walking as a Christian, but it seemed that I was not really getting anywhere. I don't have any kind of special talents. I am just a quiet introvert who enjoys spending time at home alone and with family. I honestly felt as though I had nothing worthy to offer and that there was nothing I could do for the Lord and His kingdom.

This has me thinking back to the time that I went hiking alone in the woods. After walking a while, I discovered that I was lost. I kept walking, not knowing where I was going, and hoping that I would find my way. I was walking for quite some time, for at least a couple of hours, and I started becoming afraid that I would not be able to find the right path to get to where I needed to be. So I stopped and looked to the heavens and raised my hands up and said, "Okay Lord, it's all You now. Lead me in the right direction!" I then turned toward the direction that I felt the Lord was leading me in and started walking. In just a few short minutes later, I recognized where I was! The Lord answered my prayer and showed me which way to go. When I felt as if I was lost and didn't know what my purpose in His kingdom was, I looked to the heavens and prayed for direction. I did a lot of praying about this and I finally got my answer. When I got my answer, I started walking in my purpose, letting the Lord lead me all the way.

I want you to know that if you woke up this morning and have breath in your lungs, then God still has a purpose for you on this Earth. It does not matter how young or old you are. The Lord can use anyone with a willing, obedient heart. Moses was 80 years old when God called him to lead the Israelites out of Egypt. Mary was a young teenager when she was told that she would give birth to Jesus. They were both obedient to God, and so He was able to use them in a mighty way. Stay in close connection to the Lord and keep faithfully serving Him until He reveals to you what His purpose for you is. Be aware that the purpose that God has for you now may be quite different than the purpose He will have for you in the future. Be ready to follow His lead at all times.

I am quite surprised by how the Lord has chosen to use me. It is something I would not have chosen for myself, but God is not limited with what He can do if we are willing to obey. I would like to tell you about God's purpose for me and how He revealed it to me.

One night I was lying awake in bed, unable to sleep. The Lord "spoke" to me and He told me to leave my job, and then He would make His next move. Even though it was that "still, small voice" of God speaking to my conscience, it was loud and clear. I knew right away that it was the Lord speaking to me and I understood what He was saying. I had been praying for another less stressful job, but I was not expecting God to tell me to leave my job without another one already lined up. That took me very much by surprise and I really wanted to be assured that He really did tell me that before I did anything. I asked Him for a "sign", or confirmation so that I would know for sure that was really what He was telling me to do. Believe it or not, He literally gave me a sign! Our church sign had a quote on it from Corrie Ten Boom which stated, "Never be afraid to trust an unknown future to a known God". Our Pastor's sermon that day confirmed it as well. The Holy Spirit was really speaking to me in church that day and I went to the altar to pray. I knew with all my heart that the Lord really had instructed me to leave my job. As soon as Dale and I walked out of that church, I told him what the Lord had spoken to me. He told me that he was behind me one hundred percent, no matter what, so I proceeded to give my job my two weeks notice. Thankfully I have a husband who understands that when the Lord tells you to do something, you must do it. I thank God always for my husband. He is such a blessing to me. There is no one else on this earth that I'd rather do life with than Dale. He is my gift from the Lord.

It was difficult for me to leave my job of 17 years, even with the extreme stress that I had been enduring. There were several people that I knew since I first started working there and I loved them all. I was obedient, however, and did as the Lord instructed. Shortly after I gave my employer the required two weeks notice, I was awakened in the middle of the night again. I very clearly heard a voice that was almost audible that said, "Write a book." I cannot find the words to explain it, except to say that I heard the voice, but it wasn't out loud where anyone else could hear it. Once again, I knew and understood right away that it was God's voice speaking to me. When I heard this request from the Lord, I was quite surprised! My first thought was about how God was asking me to do something that I had no experience in. Writing a book is not something that I had ever even thought about actually doing. But then I realized that if He asked me to do something that I was already skilled in doing, then how could I learn to completely and totally put my trust in Him to accomplish it through me? How could He be glorified by it? I answered Him immediately and silently prayed, "Okay, Lord. I will do whatever it is you ask of me...but I don't know how to write a book. I don't even read books, except for my Bible and devotional books. If I am going to do this, I will absolutely need You to be with me every step of the way." Since writing a book was something that I had never in my life considered doing, I thought about how I didn't know where to even begin. I decided that I would have to trust God with *all* of it.

The next day, I started getting ads on my social media accounts that stated, "Self Publish Your Book." I just sat there with my mouth hanging open, and stared at it in utter amazement for a few minutes. I hadn't even told anyone about it yet, so that was my first confirmation from the Lord that this was real and He wanted me to write a book. Even though I was quite sure of what the Lord had said to me, I asked Him for some additional confirmation. I cannot explain why I asked for it, but He willingly and speedily complied with my request. Shortly thereafter, someone I did not know started commenting on all of my posts on one of my social media accounts. I started following her page so that I could see who she was. When I read her latest post, I just could not believe it. I was utterly dumbfounded. She was a young, Christian author who had just written her first book and it was about to be released. Her post said, "Who has dreams of writing a book?" Then she went on to explain that God had called her to write a book. She also stated that if God called you to do it, He will be faithful to fulfill the vision He gave to you, and He will get it done. That was all I needed to see. My confirmation from God was received and I knew at that moment that I was going to write a book!

This has been such an amazing journey so far, and I can't wait to see what God does! If you are unsure of what your purpose in God's kingdom is, look to the Lord for direction. Ask Him to show you what it is, and then be willing to act when He does, even if you don't feel qualified. If the Lord asks you to do something, He will certainly equip you to accomplish the task He has set before you. He wants us to trust and obey Him so that He can show us what He can do through us. Work at what you are called to do with all your heart and do your best, but

CHAPTER 3 - PURPOSEFULLY ALIVE IN CHRIST

remember that God is not looking for perfection. He is looking for obedience. He is looking for willing hearts so He can fulfill the purpose that He has for them. Be present, be joyful and be willing to do what the Lord asks of you.

I caution you to be vigilant though, because our enemy Satan will try to distress you, distract you and discourage you from doing the Lord's work. While I was writing about my salvation testimony earlier in this book, I believe that I may possibly have had a glimpse of the enemy trying to thwart my work. Just after I had mentioned Satan and how he tried to destroy me, my whole book just disappeared from the program I was using. There was nothing but a blank white screen. That has never happened before. I was quite distressed while I stared at that blank screen. I frantically tried to find where all my writing had gone. It was supposed to auto save, but I could not find it. I started praying and asked the Lord not to let the enemy take it all away and to please restore it. After I prayed, my book somehow mysteriously reappeared. I was so relieved that all of what I had written was not forever lost! It was so very strange but I was so thankful that the Lord restored what the enemy tried to take away. The enemy has also been trying very hard to distract me from writing. I refuse to let him stop me from doing what God has asked me to do.

"Be sober, be vigilant; because your adversary the devil, as a roaring lion, walketh about, seeking whom he may devour." ~1 Peter 5:8

A few nights ago, I was awakened from my sleep several times, and each time I kept hearing that "still, small voice" saying, "But the Lord is with me like a Mighty Warrior!" It was also my first thought when I woke up the next morning. When the enemy comes knocking, send Jesus to answer the door. The battle is the Lord's to fight. Never forget that the enemy is no match for our great and mighty God. Keep praying and stay in God's Word. The more you read the Bible and know God's truth and keep it in your heart, the easier it will be for you to recognize the lies of the enemy.

I certainly do not want to give the enemy any glory whatsoever, but believe me when I say this: he is a master of lies and deception. Sometimes what he tells you sounds like truth, or is a partial truth, but he twists it ever so slightly to trick you into believing the lie. He will also do his best to distract you with so much busyness that pretty soon you are drifting away from God. It may even be work that you are doing for the Kingdom, but you are doing so many things and are stretched so thin that you are stressed out and tired and you have no time to be alone with the Lord. That is why I have a daily ritual of prayer and studying my Bible and devotionals first thing in the morning, before I do anything else. It fills my "spiritual tank" for the day, equipping me to have a better walk with the Lord. The devil has no power over you while you are abiding in Christ Jesus. Once you start drifting away and fall into sinful behavior, the enemy will step in and use it against you. Run away from sin as fast as you can and run toward Jesus. There is no safer place to be.

If you are a Christian, you may at times have trouble discerning between God's voice and Satan's voice. There are a few ways to know the difference. The first way to know is that God's voice will never contradict His commandments and His Word. Satan will attempt to lure you away from God's commandments, as he did with Adam and Eve. Secondly, God's voice will give you a sense of peace and clear direction, and Satan's voice will create anxiety and confusion. Also, God's voice is gentle and loving. Satan's voice is demanding and condemning and attempts to make you feel discouraged or worthless. God usually speaks when we are consciously seeking Him in prayer and Satan usually speaks with sudden intrusions into our thoughts. Learn to know the difference so that the enemy does not lure you into believing his lies.

Chapter 4 - In Unity and Forgiveness We Thrive

Unity in the church is also something that the enemy will do his best to destroy. He will use people to create conflict and stir up strife. Hating our brothers and sisters is not acceptable in the eyes of God. We must stand together and not allow it to happen. It is the Lord's will that we walk in fellowship with our brothers and sisters. We are all human and we all make mistakes, but forgiveness is something that God went to great lengths to provide when He sent His Son to die on that cross at Calvary. Shouldn't we be willing to grant the same grace, mercy and forgiveness to others that God has given to us?

1 John 3:14-16 says, "We know that we have passed from death unto life, because we love the brethren. He that loveth not his brother abideth in death. Whosoever hateth his brother is a murderer: and ye know that no murderer hath eternal life abiding in him. Hereby perceive we the love of God, because he laid down his life for us: and we ought to lay down our lives for the brethren."

A new believer is especially vulnerable to the attacks of the enemy, as I found out for myself. His goals are to separate us from the body of Christ, to keep us from growing in the

CHAPTER 4 - IN UNITY AND FORGIVENESS WE THRIVE

Lord, and to keep us from spreading the gospel. Satan means "slanderer". He is the father of lies and there is no truth in him. He uses lies and slander to separate us from each other and from God. The enemy is relentless in his pursuit of our destruction. We have to learn to recognize when he is inserting his loathsome lies into our minds and *"take captive every thought to the obedience of Christ."* (*2 Corinthians 10:5*)

When I first became a born-again believer in Christ and started coming to church, the assaults began. Every Sunday morning before the worship service began, there were two women who stood nearby and talked behind their hands or their papers that they were holding, and stared straight at me the whole time. They made it quite obvious that they were talking about me. I already felt very alone, since I didn't know anyone. I am an introvert and quite shy if I don't know someone. It kept going on and on, week after week, and finally I made the decision to move to another church because I felt so unwelcome. The Sunday morning that I had planned to go to the new church with a friend, the Holy Spirit was really speaking to my heart. I felt very strongly that He was telling me that I was not to go to the new church, and that I was to stay at my current church. I couldn't ignore what I felt I was being told, so I obeyed His voice and stayed. When I arrived at my church that morning, I sat in my normal spot on the end of the pew. I noticed that there was a woman and her husband seated all the way at the opposite end of the same pew. The Holy Spirit must have been speaking to the woman, because she got up and sat right next to me. Her husband looked quite confused, still seated down on the other end, not knowing why his wife had moved. She hugged me tightly and then started talking to me. She sat right next to me for the whole service. That hug really felt like a hug from God. I was obedient to His command to stay and He blessed me for it. I cried through the whole praise and worship portion of the service, and the tears are flowing right now as I write this. I didn't realize at the time what all this meant. All I knew was that God was involved and it drew me closer to Him.

The assaults from the enemy continued for the next couple of years, however. The two women and some others continued to talk behind my back, and said things that they apparently thought to be true, but weren't. The only conclusion that I can come to is that Satan whispered his lies, and they believed them. But they didn't know my heart. I am so thankful that God knew my heart, though. The Lord kept reminding me over and over to be still and He would fight for me. God is so faithful. He did fight for me, just as He said He would. That was a very difficult time for me, especially since I was a new believer, but I believe it was a time of testing. If you are a Christian, you will experience those times of testing of your faith through enduring trials. God allows us to endure these trials not only to draw us closer to Him, but also to refine us. It allows us to see our weaknesses so that we can cry out to the Lord for help. It also teaches us patience as we endure it and wait for the outcome. How will you respond when you are tested? Will you run away from God or will you draw nearer to Him? When you persevere in times of testing, it will result in maturing spiritually.

Something significant that I learned during that time was forgiveness. I had to forgive them, even though they weren't even aware that I knew what they were doing. A well-timed sermon about this subject from our Pastor really helped with

CHAPTER 4 - IN UNITY AND FORGIVENESS WE THRIVE

that. Forgiveness is hard, but it really is necessary for you and your own peace. Holding onto the hurt that you feel is only destroying you, not the other person.

"And be ye kind one to another, tenderhearted, forgiving one another, even as God for Christ's sake hath forgiven you." ~Ephesians 4:32

God sent His own son into the world to die a horrible death on a cross so that we could be forgiven of our sin debt. He wants us to be able to forgive others as He forgave us. Sometimes forgiveness comes easier than at other times. Sometimes, the hurt will creep back in and you have to ask the Lord for the strength to forgive all over again. I still struggle with forgiveness sometimes, but I make a conscious decision to pray and ask the Lord for help. Then I lay it all at the feet of Jesus, and in return, He gives me His peace.

In enduring that situation, I have learned something else very important. We should never assume that we know what is in someone else's heart. Looks can be very deceiving, and the only ones who truly know what you are thinking and feeling are yourself and God. If you have a concern about someone, the best thing you can do is pray about it and leave everything to the Lord. If you feel that a Christian is engaging in sinful behavior that will hurt themselves and others, go to them in love and speak to them about it. Let the truth come from their own lips, and do not rely on what you may have unintentionally conjured up in your own mind as the purported truth. Spreading rumors will hurt people and God hates that. That is why He kept telling me to be still and that He would fight for me. It was difficult to be still but I did it, and true to His word, God fought for me.

There are many verses of scripture in the Bible which warn against gossip and slander. Just doing a quick search, I have already found 32 of them, so this is a very important subject to the Lord. Let us seek to build others up and not tear them down. Let us love our brothers and sisters and not hate and destroy them with our words, for this is God's will for us. Let us be the ones who let the gossip die as soon as it hits our ears.

"Death and life are in the power of the tongue: and they that love it shall eat the fruit thereof." ~Proverbs 18:21

Chapter 5 - The Many Ways He Speaks

The Lord speaks to us in many ways. One of the ways that He speaks to us is by His still, small voice speaking to our conscience. Some of the other ways that He speaks is through Scripture, through the conviction of the Holy Spirit, through other people, and also through dreams.

The Bible is the written word of God. He speaks to us through it. It shows us the character of God and also how He wants us to live. His Word is pure, holy and infallible and we can trust in what He says. A good way to hear from God is to pray before reading your Bible and ask the Lord to speak to you through His Word. Ask Him to reveal something that He wants you to know. When I pray that before I read, He does always point to something specific in the passage that I have read for that day. Something always stands out and grabs my attention, and then I can study the meaning of it. I have had many occasions where I have asked God a question, and then picked up my Bible and started reading. What I had just asked Him was answered in His Word. I have been quite amazed by this so many times. There are also times when reading a passage of Scripture will mean something different to you than it did the last time you read it. It may speak to you differently depending on what is going on in your life at that particular point in time.

The conviction of the Holy Spirit is another way that He speaks to us. The Holy Spirit brings us under conviction of our sinful ways and makes us realize our need for a Savior, leading us to salvation through the blood of Christ. He guides us to the truth and away from sin. He leads us in the way of righteousness and prompts us to do acts of good will toward others. When we act on those promptings, not only are others blessed, but we are blessed as well. The Holy Spirit is also our Comforter, and comforts us in times of trouble and distress.

Sometimes God will speak to us through people. For example, a Pastor may preach a sermon that is perfect for a situation that you are going through. It may also be a friend, family member or co-worker who speaks the message to you. I have an example later on in this book of how God used me to speak a message of comfort to a grieving friend.

God can also speak through dreams. I had a situation where the Lord was speaking to me through all of those ways. It was when I was still a relatively new Christian, about two years after I accepted Jesus as my Lord and Savior. One night I had a very vivid dream that I got up in front of my whole church and gave my salvation testimony. That was a very frightening thought for me, as I am a very shy person who also has a fear of public speaking. In my heart I just knew that dream was God telling me to share my testimony with the church. A couple of days later, our Pastor told us that he was going to start bringing people up to share their testimonies on Sunday mornings. He said that a testimony can be a powerful thing and so he wanted the congregation to share their stories. My jaw dropped when I heard that, since I had just had that dream a couple of nights before! If you have a fear of public speaking, then you can well understand how terrified I was at just the thought of getting up in front of everyone. I struggled for probably about two months, wanting to do it but being too afraid. The Holy Spirit kept convicting me about it and I kept seeing verses of scripture with the theme, "Trust Me."

I finally got up the courage to go and speak to Pastor Phillips about it. I recall the big grin that he got on his face when I told him that God wanted me to share my testimony! He shared a story with me about how when he was a new Christian, God also told him to go up in front of his church and share his testimony. He was nervous about it too, and doesn't really remember what he said, but he was obedient and did it. He gave me some good advice and then told me to let him know when I was ready. I struggled for probably another three or four weeks before I finally came in one Sunday morning and told him I was ready.

Thankfully, he called me up to speak in the beginning of the service because waiting until the end would have been sheer torture for me. I cannot even begin to explain how nervous I was when I walked up to that altar. My voice and my whole body were shaking like crazy. When I started speaking and telling my story, it was almost like an "out of body" experience. It is difficult to explain, but it was almost as if it wasn't me up there talking. There is no doubt in my mind that God was there with me and He was giving me the words to speak. There is no way that I would have been able to do that without the Lord's help. I was so relieved after that was over! What I learned from that experience is that when God tells me to do something, I need to obey and do it immediately without delay. I could have saved myself a lot of stress and anxiety if I had just done what He asked me to do right away. I also learned to trust Him. If He asks me to do something, He will equip me with whatever I need to do it. He will be with me. He will not tell me to do something and then say, "See you later!" He is showing me that right now at this moment as I am writing this book. I pray each time that I sit down to write, and the Lord has been with me every step of the way.

Another way that God speaks to us is through His creation. Just look around you! Look at the multitude of stars in the sky and the beautiful, ever changing clouds. Look at the rich, vibrant colors of the sunrise and sunset. Look at the majestic beauty of the mountains and valleys; and the rivers, lakes and oceans. Look at the colorful, fragrant flowers. Look at the trees. How amazing are the trees? So many shapes and sizes with magnificently hued foliage, all reaching and climbing toward the heavens.

Up until a few years ago, I did not like the trees in the wintertime. They just looked so dead to me, lacking their warmer weather adornment of beautiful leaves. Let me tell you what changed my mind. One winter day I was driving on the long, winding road that goes into the park. As I was driving, something that is absolutely astounding happened. I was looking up at the leafless, dead looking trees, pondering how I didn't like what I was seeing. They looked so bare and

CHAPTER 5 - THE MANY WAYS HE SPEAKS

barren, devoid of life. Suddenly, it was as if a veil had literally been lifted from before my eyes! At that moment, I saw the trees just as I believe God sees them. I saw them as magnificent, exquisite works of art. They suddenly looked so beautiful to me, each one grand and lovely in its own way. They no longer looked like dead, barren timber. They were alive! There are absolutely no words in this universe that could ever explain that moment. I remember that tears of joy flooded my eyes at the thought that God would choose to show me such a glorious, amazing thing. What a beautiful, unexpected blessing it was, one that I will never forget.

He really revealed something significant to me that day. He doesn't see beauty as we see it. Something such as those bare, winter trees that we may see as ugly or unattractive, He sees as His beautiful creation. He also does not judge mankind the same way that we do.

"But the LORD said unto Samuel, Look not on his countenance, or on the height of his stature; because I have refused him: for the LORD seeth not as man seeth; for man looketh on the outward appearance, but the LORD looketh on the heart." ~1 Samuel 16:7

How wonderful it would be if we saw others by their heart and not their appearance, just as God does. Let's take that one step further, and imagine if we could see ourselves as God sees us. We tend to be critical of our own physical appearance, but that is not what God is concerned with. God is concerned with our heart for loving others, with our character, and with our motives and actions. He is looking for our love, devotion, and obedience to Him.

When God sent His son Jesus into the world, he was not an attractive man. Isaiah 53:2 says, *"For he shall grow up before him as a tender plant, and as a root out of a dry ground: he hath no form nor comeliness; and when we shall see him, there is no beauty that we should desire him."* God did not want anyone to follow Jesus because of what He looked like. He wanted Him to be followed because of the truth of who He was - The Son of God; the holy, sinless Messiah who came to take away the sins of the world. In Matthew 11:29, Jesus said that He is "meek and lowly of heart". If Jesus was meek and lowly of heart, shouldn't we be as well? How can we learn to follow Him if we magnify and glorify ourselves and are filled with pride? If we are full of ourselves, how can we possibly be filled with Christ? Our prayer should be, "Lord, empty me of myself so that I can be filled with You." Jesus was not the picture of physical beauty as many paintings and artwork portray Him. His beauty goes so much deeper than that. His perfect love and sinless ways are what make Him so beautiful. He was meek and lowly of heart. He was obedient to the Father and willingly died on that cross for our sins. There is no love that is more beautiful than that.

"Greater love hath no man than this, that a man lay down his life for his friends." ~John 15:13.

Chapter 6 - Becoming a Prayer Warrior

I think that I really started becoming a prayer warrior when my daughter was pregnant with my second granddaughter Emma. She had a normal, uneventful pregnancy with my first granddaughter Sophia. Sophia was one of those healthy babies with the big, adorable chubby cheeks! Emma was a different story. She was very tiny in the womb and wasn't growing normally as she should have been. The doctor seemed quite concerned about her lack of growth and had my daughter coming in weekly for ultrasounds to check on her progress. Ashley barely looked pregnant nearly up until the end of her pregnancy. I prayed very hard for that baby girl, day and night. Every time I was at church I was at the altar, at the foot of the cross, praying and crying out to God.

Then one day Ashley called me up, very upset about the baby's progress, or lack thereof. As soon as I got off the phone, I bowed my head and started praying fervently for this tiny baby and asking the Lord to sustain her and make her grow. When I finished praying, I looked up and looked at my computer screen. What I saw next was a quote from Shakespeare that said, "Though she be but little, she is fierce." As soon as I saw that, I knew in my heart that she was going to be okay. I really and truly felt as though God was telling me not to worry and that baby Emma was a fierce little fighter and she was going to make it. I felt more at peace after that, but I never stopped praying for her. I also kept seeing a verse of scripture over and over during that time. It was Jeremiah 32:27:

"Behold, I am the Lord, the God of all flesh: is there anything too hard for me?"

I found great comfort in that verse because I knew that God was in control of that child that He was knitting together in her mother's womb. Our God is all powerful and has no limitations, so there is nothing that is too difficult for Him. He reminded me quite often of that, so I kept those words in my heart and I remembered them whenever I would start to worry.

Praise God, our beautiful, tiny little Emma Faith was born healthy. Thankfully she was big enough at birth to keep her out of the neonatal intensive care unit. She was born very quickly though, and my daughter barely made it to the hospital before she gave birth! That tiny girl surely is a fierce little one who made a quick entrance into this world and into our hearts.

Being a prayer warrior can be a very powerful thing. In order to be an effective prayer warrior though, you must have a clean heart. Come before God and ask Him if there is any unrepentant sin that needs to be brought to your attention. Ask for forgiveness and repent of whatever He brings to your mind. Once your mind and heart are right with God, He will then hear your prayers. If you have a very important and challenging prayer, fasting and praying is a powerful way to bring about a breakthrough. Fasting is powerful because we are denying and humbling ourselves, and it shows our total surrender to God. We are relying on His strength, not our own. Another powerful way to pray is praying Scripture. Find a verse of Scripture that applies to the situation that you will be praying about. Personalize it and turn it into a prayer. Praying God's Word back to Him is a very effective form of prayer, which I do quite often. There is also another very powerful form of prayer, and that is praying in agreement with others. Jesus said that if two or three believers come together and pray in agreement, God the Father will hear and answer their prayer.

"Again I say unto you, That if two of you shall agree on earth as touching any thing that they shall ask, it shall be done for them of my Father which is in heaven. For where two or three are gathered together in my name, there am I in the midst of them." ~Matthew 18:19-20

Chapter 7 - Shining Like a Diamond

Our lives should be about finding joy in the wondrous pursuit of Jesus, and that joy should be the reflection of His glorious light within us, radiating brightly for the whole world to see. When you decide to let go and give all of your burdens to the Lord, it will relieve you of your stress, fear and worry. Once those things have been escorted out of your mind and your heart, that will open up the door for joy to enter. When that joy has entered and you keep filling your soul with Jesus through praise, prayer and the reading of His Word, it will bubble up within you and overflow. Others will start to notice your "joy shine." You probably know someone who just exudes joy. It's almost as if they are radiating sunshine through every pore of their being. That kind of joy can be attained through the peace and love of Christ.

I believe that negative emotions such as fear and anxiety will usually appear when we are not trusting in God and who He is. He is our Provider, our Healer, our Protector, our Comforter. He fights our battles, gives us wisdom, and is always there for us. He will never leave us. He tells us all of these things in the Bible. When we truly and fully trust in Him for all of these things, He gives us peace and freedom from those negative or fearful thoughts that take root in our minds. He is in control of every situation and there is nothing too hard for Him. God tells us many times in the Bible, "Do not fear." He wants us to know that He is bigger than anything that life can throw at us and that He is with us like a Mighty Warrior. When we go through hard things, He is there to comfort us and give us the strength to endure. When you truly believe that, it makes it easier to let go of fear and negativity.

Get into the mindset of praying and releasing all that is not well with your soul into the very capable hands of God as soon as you start to feel stressed or overwhelmed. God does not sleep and He is always working on your situation. He knows what is best for you, and more importantly, what is best to accomplish His will for the furthering of His Kingdom. In order to help keep negative thoughts and feelings from fighting their way back in, remember God's word and keep it in your heart. One verse of scripture which comes to mind is Philippians 4:8, which says:

"Finally, brethren, whatsoever things are true, whatsoever things are honest, whatsoever things are just, whatsoever things are pure, whatsoever things are lovely, whatsoever things are of good report; if there be any virtue, and if there be any praise, think on these things."

I am reminded of a situation that I had encountered about a year and a half ago that exhibits how God enables His presence in our lives to help us shine our "joy shine". My husband and I were traveling up to Long Island to visit with family, and somewhere along the way during our 4 hour journey, I looked down to notice that the diamond from my engagement ring was missing. After my initial feeling of dismay at this discovery, I felt the Holy Spirit speaking to me. I felt that the Lord was saying to me, "You do not need a diamond to shine. With my joy in your heart, you can shine brighter than a million diamonds!" I replied, "Okay Lord, I hear you and I will do my best to shine your light for all to see!" Over the next several months I spent many hours out in that car with a flashlight looking for the lost diamond. It was from the ring that my husband gave to me when he proposed to me. It had a great sentimental value and so I really wanted it back. Each time I searched for it, I prayed, "Okay Lord, I know if you want me to have it back, you will give it back to me in your timing, when You are ready." I prayed that prayer many times, and I truly believed in what I was praying.

Seven months later, we went over to my daughter's house so that Dale could help them replace the tail lights on their vehicle. When that was accomplished and we were leaving, I got into our car and accidentally put my arm down on Dale's glasses which were sitting on the center console. One of the lenses popped out and fell in the back somewhere. So I got out of the car and opened the back door and began looking for the missing lens. I looked down on the floor, and sitting right there in front of me was my diamond! It was sitting there just as if it was placed there for me to find. I could not believe my eyes! The diamond that I had searched and searched for was found! I knew in my heart that it was God that gave it back to me, and I realize now that He surprised me with it when I wasn't expecting it. I was so filled with joy at this wonderful discovery that I told my husband that I felt like the woman in the parable in the Bible that lost her silver coin. She lit a candle, searched and swept the house until she found it. When she found it, she was so filled with joy that she called her friends and neighbors over to rejoice with her. That parable was explaining about the joy of the angels in Heaven when a sinner repents. That is the kind of inexplicable joy that I felt in that moment.

The next day in church, our Pastor told us to turn to the Book of Luke, chapter 16 for the reading of the Word. After I turned there, I glanced over at the previous page to Luke, chapter 15 and saw the parable of the woman and the lost silver coin! I turned to my husband and excitedly pointed to it, because I had just mentioned it to him the previous evening when I found the diamond. This confirmed to me that God had indeed returned that diamond to me, although I already knew that. He showed me the joy that He was speaking of, and how that joy in my heart can make me shine brighter than a million diamonds. That diamond means so much more to me now. I already loved it because my husband gave it to me, but now I love it even more. God gave it back to me, and He showed me something valuable that I will be reminded of every time I see it. It reminds me to shine the light of Jesus in all that I do for all to see.

Chapter 8 - He Hears Me!

I have found that the Lord will usually show me in some way, big or small, that He hears me when I pray fervently about something. Sometimes it is a symbolic message, such as in the case of baby Emma and also the cross of sticks on the ground when I was praying for my friend. At times a pastor or friend has spoken a verbal message to me. Sometimes it is a feeling of inexplicable peace, the peace that passes all understanding. I have also heard songs after praying that perfectly described the situation I was praying for. The same with scripture. Have you ever prayed about something and then read a verse of scripture that answers a question or gives you hope, peace or faith? I have had it happen more times than I can remember. It is such a wonderful feeling, knowing that the Almighty God hears your prayers and then responds by letting you know that He is working on your situation.

As an example, one day I was praying fervently to the Lord for strength. I don't recall the situation I was praying about, but when I was done praying, I remember the next thing that I saw was a devotional that had four Bible verses about strength. The first one happened to be my favorite Bible verse, Psalm 28:7 -

CHAPTER 8 - HE HEARS ME!

"The Lord is my strength and my shield; my heart trusted in him and I am helped: therefore my heart greatly rejoiceth; and with my song will I praise him."

The other three were:

"Finally, my brethren, be strong in the Lord, and in the power of his might." ~Ephesians 6:10

"I can do all things through Christ which strengtheneth me." ~Philippians 4:13

"But be not thou far from me, O Lord: O my strength, haste thee to help me." ~Psalms 22:19

He answered my prayer through scripture.

Sometimes it seems that He isn't answering your prayers, but that doesn't mean that He didn't hear you. If you are abiding in Him and obeying His word, He will hear your prayers.

"For the eyes of the Lord are over the righteous, and his ears are open unto their prayers: but the face of the Lord is against them that do evil." ~ 1 Peter 3:12

He may not answer them in the way that you would like Him to but He will answer them in His way, in His timing, and according to His infinite wisdom. God's ways are perfect, and there is amazing peace in knowing that. God sees the big picture, not just the current one. He knows how to work everything out for your good and the good of His Kingdom.

Even though your situation may not turn out the way that you want it to, keep the faith and have peace in the knowledge that it is God's good and perfect will for you.

I wrote that last section two days ago. Today has been an awesome and amazing day because God really gave me some confirmation about what I last wrote about the other day a couple of times already this morning. When I woke up, I felt as though the Lord was saying to me, *"The Lord is with me like a Mighty Warrior."* Immediately after I had that thought, I saw that exact scripture posted on a social media website. It is from Jeremiah 20:11. I then sat down and started to pray about a situation that I feel that the Holy Spirit has been warning me about. I was praying fiercely about it because I believe that Satan is trying to mess with my family. When I got done praying, I picked up my Bible for my morning reading and went to turn to the page where I last left off. The bookmark fell out of the Bible and it opened to a different page. Amazingly, the scripture that it opened to was EXACTLY what I had just prayed about! It confirmed what I believed was happening and in that passage was God's assurance that He heard my prayer and that He is working on it. Our God is mighty and powerful, and I am praising Him with a joyful heart for all He is doing in my life.

There are times when we pray for something for days, weeks, months or even years before we get an answer. Don't give up when it seems as if God is not answering. You can be assured that He heard you (unless you have some unrepentant sin in your life). His timing is always perfect and while you are waiting, He is working. If you keep this in mind, you can

CHAPTER 8 - HE HEARS ME!

remain at peace while He works on your situation. Sometimes while you are waiting, the Lord is working on you. Perhaps you are not ready for what you prayed for. If that is the case, He will wait until you are ready. If God is making you wait, ask Him to reveal to you what He wants you to know, or change, or do in the meantime. I have found in my own experience that God usually will not change my circumstances until I learn what He wants me to learn from it first. Only when I have finally gleaned the lesson He set out for me to discover and embrace, will I see a breakthrough and a change in my circumstances.

One such time that I prayed persistently for something and waited for quite some time for an answer was when I was praying to lose weight. Due to a malfunctioning thyroid and slow metabolism, I had gained quite a lot of weight. I wanted so desperately to lose the excess weight and so I began praying about it. My weight just kept creeping up and it was a very distressing thing for me. None of my clothing fit me anymore and I just wanted an easy way to get rid of all of the extra weight I had acquired. I did some research on some different weight loss supplements, but I couldn't find anything that showed consistent results with other people. I wanted an easy way out, some "magic pill" or something to make the weight disappear effortlessly. But that is not what God wanted. So I changed my thoughts and my attitude about it and I started praying for the Lord to show me how to be a good steward of this body that He created. I asked Him to teach me how to eat healthy and how to lose this excess weight so that I could stop feeling so tired and worn out all the time. I was tired of having to take naps every day and I had other issues which were exacerbated by carrying around the extra weight. I also wanted to be able to do simple things like paint my toenails and breathe at the same time! I stopped asking Him to make it easy and I told Him that if He would show me how to be healthy, I would do it. I made a promise that I would do whatever He instructed me to and I would stick with it. That is when my breakthrough came.

The Lord pointed me toward a couple of wonderful ladies who had great success with a weight loss program and I really felt as though He was telling me that was what I needed to pursue. I decided to take the plunge and try it. It is not just a diet, but is truly a lifestyle change. I began losing weight immediately, and so that encouraged me to continue. It is now one year later and I have lost 85 pounds. I had to totally change the way that I eat, from the types of foods to the portion sizes. I keep track of everything that I eat and stay within my allowance for the day. I realize that I can never go back to the way I used to eat because I will gain the weight back. There are times that I struggle with wanting to eat something that I shouldn't, so I have to call on the Lord to give me strength to resist that urge and eat something healthy instead.

You can see that when I changed my attitude about the whole issue, God answered my prayers. He didn't want me to have an easy way out, even though He could have made it easy if He had wanted to. He wanted me to work for it, because it taught me the proper way to eat healthy and showed me what I was doing wrong. If He had given me an easy way to lose all that weight, I likely would have just gained it back again and I would not have learned anything. I am so thankful that God, in His infinite wisdom, chose to make me wait until I changed my thinking. It really was an amazing blessing.

Chapter 9 - Tossing Mountains Into the Sea

I have discovered that if the Lord wants you to do something, He will move mountains to make sure it gets done. There was a time several years back when there was a "Parent Workshop" that was being taught by the Youth Pastor at our church. I hadn't actually planned on going, but on the day that it was to begin I had a very strong feeling that the Lord was telling me to go to it. At the time I was working a split shift because it was one of my days to work remotely from home. With the split shift, I worked half of my hours in the morning and then the other half in the evening. It was too late for me to request the time off and so there was no way for me to get off work early to attend that workshop. So I foolishly told the Creator of the Universe, "Sorry, I can't go, I have to work." Silly me! I was still a new Christian at the time and I was not yet aware of what God is capable of. He kept urging me to go, despite my refusal. He wasn't letting me off the hook about it, so finally I said, "Okay Lord. If you really want me to go, then make a way for me to go." Well, about 15 or 20 minutes later, I received an email saying that my schedule had been changed for that day and I was working a straight 9 to 5 shift instead of a split shift. I would be getting off work at 5:00 pm and so I would indeed be able to do what the Lord had asked me to do. I do not know how He changed my schedule, but you can bet that I was at that "Parent Workshop" that evening! I kept that email with the schedule change, and I still have it to this day as proof of God's mighty power to do the impossible.

When God wants you to do something, He will make a way when there seems to be no way. There is nothing that He cannot do and nothing is too hard for Him. I now know never to doubt God and His ability to move a supposed mountain. He will take that mountain and cast it into the midst of the sea! How awesome and amazing is that? Nothing and no one can stop God from accomplishing His will. And when He moves that mountain out of the way, we absolutely must move forward and accomplish the task that He has set before us. Obedience is integral in our relationship with the Lord. We must learn to put our own aspirations, desires and comfort aside and run wholeheartedly toward Jesus with our arms and hearts wide open to receive the tasks He chooses to bestow upon us. I find it truly amazing and exciting that the Lord God Almighty, maker of Heaven and Earth, wants to use us to accomplish His glorious purpose. How could we ever say no to Him? We truly should not refuse to obey the Lord and whatever He asks of us.

Everything that we do, everything that we go through, everything that we are, every single second of our lives, is all about Jesus and His Kingdom. He can do great and mighty things through humble and surrendered people. That is essentially what it takes for the Lord to use us to accomplish his goals - a willing, humble and surrendered heart. The rest will be supplied by the Lord. He will move those mountains, and He will do supernatural things to help you, but you have to trust in Him and His mighty power. Do not fear the journey because He will be with you and He will never leave you. You are covered by His amazing grace.

Chapter 10 - A Dreamer Dreaming Dreams

God can speak to us through dreams. Back when I was a new Christian, I had a few dreams that I feel sure were from God. They were very intense dreams and I cannot even begin to explain how real they felt. It was as if I was actually experiencing what was in those dreams. The first of the dreams that I had began with a booming sound and the earth shaking, which was an earthquake. Then the moon turned blood red and the sun went black and it was dark. Later on in that same dream, there was fire everywhere and the grass was burned up. The last thing that I remember at the very end of the dream, was a very intense heat. The intense heat kept getting hotter and hotter until I couldn't take it anymore. The whole earth was burning up. It was then that I woke up, my heart racing because that dream just seemed so real! The next day, I told my daughter about it and she informed me that those are things that happen in the Book of Revelation in the Bible. I had not read about that yet so I had no knowledge of it as of the time of that dream. I had no idea why I had that dream, but I truly felt that it was from the Lord. The next day I prayed about it, and after I did, I felt prompted to read the book of Acts. So I got out my Bible and started reading. I was quite shocked when I

CHAPTER 10 - A DREAMER DREAMING DREAMS

got to Acts 2:20, which said,

"The sun shall be turned into darkness, and the moon into blood, before the great and notable day of the Lord come."

I believe that was the Lord's confirmation to me that the dream was indeed from Him. After experiencing that dream, I most certainly found and read about those events in the Book of Revelation. Somehow I feel as though I have experienced some of that book through that dream.

In another dream that I had when I was still a new believer, I was in a large empty white room with a fierce lion. I was scared to death of the lion until I heard Jesus say, *"Fear not, for I am the mighty Lion of Judah."* Once I trusted that it was Jesus there and He was protecting me, I was not afraid anymore. I was safe and secure. Once again, this dream was so intensely real that I feel certain that it was from God. I had heard the term "Lion of Judah" before but I was totally unaware of it's meaning and that it referred to Jesus. Jesus told me in that dream that He is the Lion of Judah. He also told me not to be afraid because He wanted me to trust in Him to defend me. The morning after I had that dream, I started researching it on the internet and found out that Jesus indeed is referred to as the Lion of Judah in the Book of Revelation 5:5. I did not realize until just now at this moment while writing this that both of these dreams refer to the Book of Revelation in their meaning and context.

I recall telling a Pastor about the first dream and he told me that Jesus said, "What I tell you in secret, shout from the housetops." That is from Matthew 10:27 which says:

"What I tell you in darkness, that speak ye in light: and what ye hear in the ear, that preach ye upon the housetops."

I believe that the Lord has very clearly been telling me to write about these dreams because He keeps reminding me of them. After I started writing about them, I saw something which stopped me in my tracks. What I saw refers to a verse of scripture from Job 33:14-15 (New Living Translation). It said, *"For God speaks again and again, though people do not recognize it. He speaks in dreams, in visions of the night, when deep sleep falls on people as they lie in their beds."* The next line verse 16 says, *"He whispers in their ears and terrifies them with warnings."* Was He giving me a warning that He wants me to shout from the housetops? I honestly don't know God's purpose for those dreams, but I do know that He told me about things that I did not know.

I did some research on how to know if a dream is from God. One thing that indicates that it is a God-dream is that it contains something that you wouldn't ordinarily know, or contains information about a future time. I believe that this would apply to both of the dreams that I described, since they are both from the Book of Revelation (future time) and told me information that I was not aware of. Another indicator is that you may receive a confirming sign, such as a Pastor preaching the same message that you received from your dream. Something else that I learned is that we should ask ourselves if this is something that Jesus would say. Also, does it point you toward Jesus and Scripture? There seems to be a lot of symbolism in dreams, just as there is in Scripture. In my dream about the lion, the lion symbolized Jesus, the Lion of Judah.

CHAPTER 10 - A DREAMER DREAMING DREAMS

God speaks in dreams at times because we just have so much going on during the day that we are not still and quiet enough to hear Him when He is trying to tell us something. In my own experience though, when God has something important to say to me, He will wake me up in the middle of the night. That is how He told me to leave my job, then to write a book, and also how He told me the title of the book. He has also woken me up at night to tell me specific things that He wants me to write about. If you are lying awake at night unable to sleep, pray and tell Him what's on your heart. Then be still and listen. He may have something important to tell you.

As I was praying this morning, the Lord brought to my mind something that I have a very strong feeling that He wants me to include in this chapter. He reminded me of a time back when I was a new believer, and I was out in my neighborhood walking. That is something that I did every day back then. I listened to worship music and walked around the whole neighborhood. I called these walks my "worship walks". In the middle of my walk, I had a "vision" of sorts. I would describe it as sort of a daydream. In this vision I saw a friend from church, standing in a very specific spot in the neighborhood store. Later on that day, I went to that store to go shopping. When I arrived and walked into the store, I saw that same friend standing in the exact spot that I saw them in that vision. Not only that, but everywhere I went in that store, we kept unintentionally crossing paths and ending up in the same aisles. I don't exactly know why that happened, but I do know that I truly felt at the time that the Lord was telling me to pray for this person. I believe that this may have been God's way of bringing this person to my attention. This was the same friend that I mentioned earlier that I was praying for and then I saw the cross of sticks lying on the ground. That person was about to go through a major storm in their life, and I see now why the Lord wanted me to pray for them. If someone keeps coming to your mind or crossing paths with you, pray for them. You never know what is going on in their life and your prayers can help immensely.

Chapter 11 - Saved For a Purpose

Have you ever had something happen that just absolutely shakes you to your core because only by the grace of God you escaped serious harm or death? This has happened to me, on more than one occasion. It has probably happened to most of us at some point in our lives. One day about 20 years ago, before I was even a born-again believer, I was in my car driving somewhere and was stopped at a traffic light. When the light turned green, something stopped me from stepping on the accelerator and going through the intersection. I cannot explain why, but I just sat there looking at the green traffic light. Something told me not to go. It was almost as if I was in a trance. Seconds later, a very large SUV pulling a boat went flying through the red light, probably going at least 70 mph. From where I was sitting on the intersecting road, I couldn't see it coming because of a hill obscuring my view. If I had proceeded through that intersection when the light turned green, I would have been killed instantly. The vehicle that went through the red light at that high rate of speed would surely have hit me directly on the driver's side.

I was so shaken, but yet so thankful. I recall very clearly that I cried and thanked God for saving me from the horrific accident that could have occurred. As I said earlier, I was not a born-again believer at that time, but somehow I still knew it was God that saved me from that accident. I felt it deeply in my heart. If He hadn't stopped that accident and I had died, I believe that I would be spending my eternity in Hell right now. What a sobering thought, yet at the same time, what a wonderful feeling that the Lord did not want me to die and end up in eternal damnation that day. He was not done with me yet. He still had plans for me. That brings to mind Jeremiah 29:11-13:

"For I know the thoughts that I think toward you, saith the Lord, thoughts of peace, and not of evil, to give you an expected end. Then shall ye call upon me, and ye shall go and pray unto me, and I will hearken unto you. And ye shall seek me and find me, when ye shall search for me with all your heart."

The Lord mercifully saved my life that day, and I did eventually call upon Him and pray to be forgiven and saved eight years ago. And here I am today, seeking Him with all my heart. My ending could have been so different. But that is not what God had planned for me. He wanted me to be saved. He wanted me to be able to worship Him, have a relationship with Him, learn about Him and even to write a book.

My heart is filled with so much gratitude and joy for all the things that He has done for me and in me. The blessings just keep flowing, and so how could I ever thank Him except to give Him all of me? My life, my heart and my praise is all for Jesus, the giver of life. The giver of not only physical life, but also spiritual life, eternal life and abundant life.

CHAPTER 11 - SAVED FOR A PURPOSE

"The spirit of God hath made me, and the breath of the Almighty hath given me life."
 ~Job 33:4

Jesus also said that He is the bread of life, and that He gives us the living water. When we believe in Him, it will be in us a well of water springing up into everlasting life. In John 10:10, this is what Jesus said:

"I am come that they might have life, and that they might have it more abundantly."

The giver of life wants us. He wants our attention and our love. He wants our lives, hearts and praise devoted to Him and focused on Him. He is the only one who is worthy of that.

It is so easy in our hectic, crazy lives to get distracted and fall away from our Creator. We have to be intentional about staying connected to Him. Praying and talking to Him throughout the day is the number one way to accomplish this. Talk to Him about every decision, about every problem, and about every joy. In all things, give thanks. There is always something to be thankful for, even the breath in your lungs. When you keep a constant line of communication open with Him and seek His will in all things, He will show up in big and mighty ways in your life because you are opening the door for Him to work on your behalf.

Chapter 12 - Let God Be God

We must remember to let God be God, and resist the urge to try to do things our own way. We do not see things the way God does, and lack the foresight to see potential problems down the road caused by our wrong decisions. Ask the Lord for His wisdom and guidance for each and every situation you encounter and He will give it to you. God's ways are perfect and are always the best ways, even though we may not understand it at the time. We may understand it at a later time, but sometimes we will not. That is okay because we do not need to understand everything that God does to know that His way is always best.

"For my thoughts are not your thoughts, neither are your ways my ways, saith the Lord. For as the heavens are higher than the earth, so are my ways higher than your ways, and my thoughts than your thoughts." ~Isaiah 55:8-9

Seek His will in all decisions and situations, and be prepared to obediently follow His instructions, confidently knowing that God knows what He is doing. He has a solution to every problem before it even comes up. You can trust Him wholeheartedly with every moment of your life.

CHAPTER 12 - LET GOD BE GOD

A few years ago, my daughter, son-in-law and their two young daughters moved away to the state of Illinois. My son-in-law felt that the Lord was leading them out there. He was offered a job and their home was sold without even putting it up for sale. The way that everything was lining up, it really and truly looked like it was God's will for them to move. I am very close to my daughter and granddaughters, and so it was extremely difficult for me to watch them leave. It was breaking my heart, and I wanted so much to try to talk them out of it. However, I knew that if it was God's will, I had to let them go. And so I put on a brave face and did my best not to let them know how heartbroken I really felt. I absolutely did not want them to move away, but I knew in my heart that I could not go against God's plan for them. I just kept praying for the Lord to help me through it and I told Him I would accept whatever His will was. It was very difficult for my daughter to leave everything and move so far away, so I did not want to make things harder on her.

On the evening of the day that they left, my husband took me out to a restaurant for dinner. As I sat there trying to eat my dinner, the reality that they were gone just hit me like a brick wall and I just broke down sobbing. I was crying so hard that I couldn't eat. Unfortunately, we were seated at one of those tables that are out in the middle of the floor, so I could not hide my face. I think that I managed to swallow a few mouthfuls of food, but I just wanted to get out of there and go home, away from all those people.

The next several months were difficult. I did a lot of praying and asking for the Lord to help me through my sadness. I felt as though there was such a hole in my life without them. I continually told the Lord that I accepted whatever His will was, but I also prayed quite fervently for Him to bring them back here. Things out in Illinois were not working out well. The job that my son-in-law was offered never happened. They strung him along for months telling him that he would have that job, but it never materialized. He worked a couple of other jobs in the interim, but ultimately things just did not work out. About 7 months after they left, they moved back to Maryland. I was absolutely overjoyed when they came back! What a wonderful blessing it is to have them back here.

The point that I am trying to make with this story is that it was obviously God's will for my daughter and her family to move to Illinois. It was also His will that things would not work out while they were out there and that they would come back here. God had a reason and a purpose for it, even though we don't understand it. Perhaps some day we will. Perhaps not. But I am confident of this one thing: The Lord was working on them in some way while they were out there. I also feel sure that He was working on me as well. One thing that I learned is that I had to submit to His will, even though I did not understand it and I did not want to let my family move so far away. I wanted to keep them here for myself, but they belong to the Lord. I hope and pray that through all of that, we learned what He wanted us to learn, and did what He wanted us to do. I'd rather not have to repeat something difficult just because I didn't get the lesson that the Lord was trying to teach me the first time. If I feel that the Lord is trying to show me something, I want to pay attention and do my best to understand the lesson expediently.

CHAPTER 12 - LET GOD BE GOD

Sometimes we don't pay attention or recognize what God wants to show us, or perhaps we just don't want to make the change that the Lord wants us to make, so He will keep us in our situation until we do. It can be painful to be stuck in a situation that you don't want to be in. When this happens, I suggest that you pray. Pray and ask God if there is something that He wants you to know, if there is a change you need to make or if there is something you should be doing while you are waiting for Him to work on your situation. Then listen for the answer and pay attention to what comes into your mind. He will answer you if you are praying earnestly. If God is trying to teach you something, He will not withhold the information that He is trying to impart to you. He is continually working in our hearts and on our character and sometimes He uses trials and tribulations to do it. He is like a potter working with clay, molding and shaping us into the mature Christians that He wants us to be. You are a work in progress, being transformed into His beautiful, wonderful masterpiece.

Chapter 13 - Devotion Takes Courage

One of the most courageous things you can ever do is to be a devoted follower of Jesus Christ. People may hate you, make fun of you and even leave you. Jesus said that would happen.

"If the world hate you, ye know that it hated me before it hated you. If ye were of the world, the world would love his own: but because ye are not of the world, but I have chosen you out of the world, therefore the world hateth you. Remember the word that I said unto you, The servant is not greater than his lord. If they have persecuted me, they will also persecute you; if they have kept my saying, they will keep yours also." ~John 15:18-20

But there is good that comes from being persecuted for Christ. We are blessed!

"Blessed are ye, when men shall hate you, and when they shall separate you from their company, and shall reproach you, and cast out your name as evil, for the Son of man's sake." ~Luke 6:22

In some countries, people are imprisoned, tortured and executed for following Christ. Thankfully we don't currently suffer that level of persecution in America. That may change

CHAPTER 13 - DEVOTION TAKES COURAGE

some day. I pray that it does not. However, when you realize how great God is and what Jesus accomplished when He paid the debt for our sins as He hung and died on the cross, you know that it is all worth it. Everything we endure in this life will be a very small price to pay to be surrounded by God's glory forever in Heaven. Jesus' death, burial and resurrection gave us back the relationship with God that we lost when Adam and Eve disobeyed God and were exiled from the Garden of Eden. Their sin separated them (and all of us) from the beautiful, close relationship they had with God. When Jesus bore our sin upon Himself on the cross, it bridged the gap that was between mankind and God. We have access to God now, when we accept His gift of salvation and repent of our sins. Yes, it does take courage to be "all in" for Christ, but you will experience Him in ways that you can't even imagine. Living for this sinful world will get you nothing in the eternal perspective, but living for Christ will get you everything that matters. This world is temporary, but Christ is eternal.

We must remind ourselves often that our time on Earth is very brief. What are we doing with that brief amount of time that we have? Are we committing it to the Lord and His Kingdom or to ourselves? I feel as though He is asking me that very question right at this moment as I am writing this. I know that my works (deeds) do not make me righteous before God and won't get me into Heaven, only my faith in Christ will. However, a changed heart will produce an active faith that will bear much fruit when we obey God and what He commands us to do. If our faith is dead and our hearts have not been changed by Christ, we will not produce any fruit and will have no desire to work for the good of His Kingdom.

"For as the body without the spirit is dead, so faith without works is dead also." ~James 2:26

Chapter 14 - A Shoebox Full of Love

I would like to tell you about a wonderful ministry from Samaritan's Purse called Operation Christmas Child. You can pack shoeboxes with gifts for children in need around the world that otherwise would not receive a Christmas gift. A lot of these children have never received a gift ever before, and seeing the joy on their faces when they receive their box is just amazing! In addition to receiving their shoebox filled with gifts, they also get to hear the message of the Gospel, and learn about how much Jesus loves them. I have read many amazing stories from people who took part in this ministry and how the child that received their box got exactly what they wanted or needed. I have a little story of my own from when I packed some shoeboxes a few years ago. I heard about the ministry and decided that I would like to pack a shoebox for a little girl. So I went about my way, looking for the perfect gifts for a little girl that would fit into the box. It was actually a lot of fun shopping for these items, and when I had bought all the fun little gifts that I could jam into that little shoebox, I proceeded to fill it with the items. When I had completed that task, I kept hearing that "still, small voice" of God telling me to also do a box for a boy and to buy a baseball for it. Well, it was November, and baseball season was over. I knew that I was going to have difficulty finding a baseball at that time of the year. This was before shopping on the internet was a big thing. I kept putting it off, but I kept "hearing" the Lord tell me to buy a baseball. I was running out of time for the shoebox collection week, so I finally went back to the store to buy the gifts for a boy. The first thing I looked for was that baseball that the Lord kept reminding me to buy. There weren't any, just as I had feared. I thought about it for a few minutes and then decided that perhaps I could get a football instead. However, I kept hearing the Lord's voice, speaking to my conscience, telling me to get a baseball. As I started to walk away from the sports aisle, I saw a random newspaper sitting on a shelf all by itself with a picture of a baseball player with an angry face, ready to throw a baseball. It was at that point that I knew that I had to go to the ends of the earth if need be to find that baseball. With some further searching I did manage to locate one at another store, along with some other baseball related items for that shoebox. I do not know who received that box, but I have absolutely no doubt whatsoever that the child that received it wanted a baseball. How humbling it is that God used me to get that ball to that child. What an awesome experience that was! I look forward to packing many more shoeboxes in the future. What an absolute blessing it is to both the givers and receivers of these gifts.

After hearing so many other amazing stories and seeing several videos of children receiving their shoebox gifts, I feel sure that God chooses the right box for each and every child that receives one. I am amazed by this and I am reminded of His goodness and how He knows the needs of each and every one of His children. He is a good Father and He gives us good things. The very best of these things that He gives us are not tangible, worldly things. The greatest of these gifts is forgiveness and salvation through the blood of His only begotten Son, Jesus. That gift demonstrates His amazing love for us that is so great and high and wide that we cannot even begin to fathom it. He also gives us wonderful things such as comfort when we're hurting, wisdom when we seek it, healing when we're sick, and companionship when we're lonely. He will never forsake us and He will never leave us. When we cry out to Him for help, He is there for us, always. What more could we ask for than such devotion from our heavenly Father?

"Every good gift and every perfect gift is from above, and cometh down from the Father of lights, with whom is no variableness, neither shadow of turning." ~James 1:17

Chapter 15 - Jesus Wept

Sometimes the Lord will use people to get a message to someone that needs to hear it. Sometimes it may be through a Pastor, sometimes through a song, or sometimes it may be a friend or loved one that brings that message to you. One morning in March 2015 as I was getting ready for church, I was thinking about how Jesus wept when His friend Lazarus died and how Jesus knows our pain when we are suffering. About five minutes later, I sat down at my computer and saw that a Pastor friend from the Philippines had posted *"John 11:35 - Jesus wept"*. I was quite astonished that I had seen that right after I had been thinking about it. Later on that evening, I was at church for our evening service and we had a business meeting. I was handed some papers with the minutes from the previous meeting. Immediately my eyes were drawn to the center of the page where it stated, *"Jesus wept."* I was floored! I truly felt that the Lord was laying this on my heart because someone needed to receive the message that Jesus knows every heartache and pain that we have, because He experienced it too. He is near to the brokenhearted and binds up their wounds. He is with us always and He heals all of our pain. He loves us so much and wants us to bring our burdens to Him so that He can bring us through whatever it is that we are going through. We need only to call on the mighty name of Jesus and then reach out and take His hand.

I believe that message was for a friend that had just lost her husband. She kept coming to my mind and I knew that she was really struggling with his loss. I can't even imagine how she felt, losing the love of her life, but Jesus knew! He wanted her to know that she could take His hand and He would lead her through it. He is our hope in the good times, but especially in the bad times. It is in the difficult times that we tend to desperately seek Him and cling to Him for comfort. He will always be there when we need Him. He will never leave us and He will never forsake us. If you put all of your hope in Him, He will heal your weary, broken, tattered heart and make it whole again.

Chapter 16 - A Door Closes, But Another Opens

When we seek God with our whole hearts, He will get involved in our lives in a big and mighty way. I often wonder why God is so good to me, but I do know that His goodness draws me closer to Him. It seems like a wonderful cycle of His goodness drawing me nearer to Him which causes me to seek Him even more. I have also come to realize that when I seek His will and His wisdom, that is when I see positive results in all manner of situations. When I try to go my own way, that is when I falter. Then I have to try again, but this time God's way. We truly must get into the habit of seeking God on every single decision and every single situation. That is most assuredly what He wants. And when that is also what we want, He will honor that with His involvement. I see this more and more in my own life. The more I seek Him and His will, the more He shows up.

Recently, my husband and I have been searching for a new home. We like our current house, however we live in a heavily wooded area and we get no sun in our yard. I also have to battle the mosquitoes that attack me every time I go outside. I very much enjoy gardening, but I am not able to do any of that with the lack of sunlight on our property. My gardening

CHAPTER 16 - A DOOR CLOSES, BUT ANOTHER OPENS

at this home has consisted only of potted plants on the back deck. I have always wanted a big, open, sunny yard with lots of grass and room to plant flower and vegetable gardens. Dale wanted to have a yard big enough to have a pole barn to use for a workshop. We discovered that we both love the Fair Hill area of Maryland, and that beautiful countryside is what drew us and our families to Maryland when we first moved to this area.

So, we started looking around for a home that would better suit what we desired. We were checking the real estate websites daily, waiting patiently for the right home to appear. I asked the Lord to choose the best home for us. We both prayed for Him to direct us to the right home and to give us the wisdom to know it was the right one when we found it. As we looked, it seemed that every time we found a home that we liked, it was right next to some high tension power lines. We did not want to live right next to those due to the health risks of the electromagnetic fields that are generated by them, so the presence of that type of power lines in close proximity immediately negated the prospect of purchasing those particular properties.

So we patiently searched, for approximately a year, when we finally came across a home that we were very interested in. It had a big beautiful open yard, with some horses on a neighboring property. The house itself was very pretty and was the style that we wanted, but it needed a lot of updating inside. We were willing to put in the time and effort to update the property, especially since the home was selling at a very good price. It was below our budget which would have left us enough money to fix it up. We prayed about it and asked God to open the door if it was the right home and close the door if this was not the right property for us. As we moved ahead and started to try to put an offer in on the house, everything seemed to be working against us. There was quite a lot of interest in this house, and the bids started rolling in. The seller would not even accept an offer from us because we would have had to make it contingent upon the sale of our current home first. That was strike one. We pursued some other avenues to try to purchase the home, but nothing was working out. We realized that God was closing the door. We were disappointed, but we realized that if God was closing that door, He had something better in mind for us. So we then picked up where we left off and continued on with our search.

One morning I was lying in bed while Dale was getting ready for work. I was praying about something that the Lord had been bringing to my attention. When I was working, I was bringing in a good amount of money and I really never gave a thought to how much I was spending. If I wanted something, I bought it. When I went grocery shopping, I never paid attention to how much I was spending on food. Now that the Lord has asked me to leave my job and write a book, I don't have all that money coming in anymore. It crossed my mind that perhaps the Lord not only wanted me to leave my job to write, but also to teach me to be a good steward of our income. So on that morning when I was praying, I promised God that I would be a better steward of the money that He provides for us. After I got done praying, I picked up my phone to check the real estate website to see if anything new had been posted. Surprisingly, there was a new listing for a house that looked like it had everything that we wanted. I was getting this feeling that this home could be "the one" and was also wondering if God had been waiting for

CHAPTER 16 - A DOOR CLOSES, BUT ANOTHER OPENS

me to make that promise I had just made before he gave it to us. I showed it to Dale before he left for work and he asked me to contact Ron, our Realtor, to schedule a showing. The listing for the house only had one photo of the outside. Most listings have several photos of the interior of the home as well. I waited for a while before calling Ron, hoping for some more pictures to be added to the listing so I could see what the inside looked like. Nothing new was added, so I contacted him and scheduled a time to go and see the home the following day since it was a Saturday and Dale would be off work.

The next day we met Ron at the home for sale and walked through it. The inside of the home was just as beautiful as the outside. It had a nice, big fenced in backyard. It also had a pole barn workshop in back, which is one of the things that Dale wanted. It was also in the Fair Hill area of Maryland that we both really loved. We decided to go home and pray about it, and we asked God for wisdom again. We wanted Him to open the door if it was the right home for us, or close it if it wasn't. I also asked Him to hold onto the house if it was the one He had chosen for us, and not let anyone else purchase it. We expressed to our Realtor that we had an interest in the home, but we felt it was overpriced. We went back to look at it again and decided that we would like to put an offer in on it, but we had some questions about some things in the home first.

A week had elapsed at this point and the home had been shown to a few other people but no one put in an offer on it yet. I believe that this was most likely because the asking price for the home was too high, and also because the listing agent did eventually put a few pictures of the interior of the home on the real estate websites, but the photos were very dark and not very good. They did not accentuate the positive attributes of the home. I believe that this all worked to our advantage.

We spent the next two weeks contemplating whether it was the right move to put in an offer on the house. We really weren't sure what to do even though we had prayed many times about it, so we sat down and started talking about whether it seemed that God was opening or closing the door on this property. We discovered that everything that had already transpired pointed towards an open door. No one else had put in a bid on it, it had everything that we wanted and needed to have in a home, and it was in the area that we both loved. Another thing that occurred during this time that truly seemed to open the door is the sale of some property that Dale owned in another state, which would enable us to purchase the new home and move into it, and then sell our old home. That would make it so much easier on us than having to sell our old home first, put all our things in storage and find temporary housing, and then move into the new home. The proceeds from the sale of the out of state property just happened to be the same amount that we needed to purchase the new house. Yet another open door.

Everything seemed to be coming together, so we made the decision to put in an offer on the house, which was $30,000 less than the asking price. We felt that it was a fair price. The sellers came back with a counter offer, which we felt was still too high. We countered back with another offer and waited for a response. While we were waiting, we decided to get some fast food since it was dinner time. We parked the car next to a nice shade tree in a parking lot and ate our food and talked about

CHAPTER 16 - A DOOR CLOSES, BUT ANOTHER OPENS

the day's events. When we were done eating, Dale went to start the car to go home and it wouldn't start. He tried several times and it just wouldn't start. We were sitting there pondering our next move and I said to him, "Maybe we aren't supposed to move from this spot right now for some reason." Just then Dale's phone rang - it was Ron our Realtor, letting us know that our offer was accepted by the sellers! We were so happy to hear that wonderful news! After speaking with Ron for a few minutes, he hung up the phone and tried to start the car again to go home and it started right up! We didn't have any problems at all with it after that. We both agree that it just really and truly felt as though that was God's signature on that whole situation. He was letting us know that He was indeed involved, and this blessing came from Him. I feel that is the most exciting thing about the whole experience! God's involvement is such an amazing and wonderful thing and nothing in this world could ever compare.

It is so very interesting to see the difference between when the Lord is closing a door and when He opens it. When He opens a door, He will not cause you to go against or contradict His Word to go through it. It seems as though when God starts opening the doors of opportunity, the floodgates open up and His blessings start flowing freely down upon us. When He closes a door, that just means that was not the right one and He has something better in mind. I have never felt that God made the wrong decision or gave me less than his best. He will never steer us in the wrong direction. He desires for us to seek His wisdom and guidance in every decision. He also desires a close, intimate relationship where we come to Him with all of our requests with praise and thanksgiving.

Chapter 17 - Giving it All to God

I am so thankful that I have such a loving God that is always there for me at every moment. He is a God that takes care of my every need and reminds me often that I don't have to worry or be in distress because He is in control and will work everything out for my good. I think back on the days before I had this close, personal relationship with Him and I do not know how I did it. I had to rely on myself to get through difficult situations. I don't ever want to do that again. That was a hard and lonely place to be. It is so very freeing to just give your burdens to the Lord and let Him work it all out.

My pastor once said that you will always be in one of three places in your life. Either you are about to enter a storm, you are currently in one, or you have just recently come out of one. The storms in this life will come, regardless of whether or not you are a Christian. The difference is that when you know Jesus, you can have peace in the midst of the storm. Close your eyes for a moment and think back to a difficult time you encountered when you did not know Jesus. I feel quite sure that that is more than likely not a good memory for you. You may have felt hopeless and helpless in your situation. Now think about what it would have been like if you had known Him and

CHAPTER 17 - GIVING IT ALL TO GOD

had a close, personal relationship with Him at that time. Think about what a difference it would have made in your situation to have the Lord to give your burdens to and pray to and ask Him for help.

"I will lift up mine eyes unto the hills, from whence cometh my help. My help cometh from the Lord, which made heaven and earth." ~Psalm 121:1-2

Back during the time when I was dealing with depression, which I struggled with for several years, I felt so all alone and the darkness just overshadowed my whole life. I felt like I was drowning and had no one to save me. I did not know Jesus back then, so I did not know where to turn or what to do. I was truly lost. I could not give my burdens to Him because I didn't have a relationship with Him. I did not have that freedom to take all those burdens and dark feelings and give them to Jesus and cling to Him for dear life. My whole life changed drastically when I found Him and His saving grace. I found out that I was not worthless because Jesus loves me so much that He died for me. My worth and my identity are in Him. He is the King and I am a precious daughter of the Star Breather.

"By the word of the Lord were the heavens made; and all the host of them by the breath of his mouth." ~Psalm 33:6

So often it seems as believers when we are experiencing difficulty in our lives, we try to handle it ourselves. However, that is not what God wants. He wants us to come to Him with all of our troubles and our worries and our disasters and just lay them at His feet and ask Him for His divine help. Even if we got ourselves into a bad situation, He can still work it out for good. Don't be afraid to pour out your heart to Him, no matter what the situation is. God longs for us to tell Him about all the big things and also the small things that concern us, and He wants to be actively involved in *all* of it. When we pray and we know that He hears us and is working it all out for us, it can truly put us in a peaceful frame of mind. Instead of trying to handle our difficulties on our own, the first thing we should do is pray and ask for the wisdom, discernment and divine assistance of the One who created us, takes care of us and loves us so much.

Chapter 18 - Let Your Light Shine!

A few weeks ago I saw a quote from an unknown author that said, "I used to be afraid of the dark until I learned that I am a light and the dark is afraid of me." Think about that - if we have the light of Jesus shining in us, the dark (Satan) is afraid of us. That is why he tries so hard to derail us. He does not want us to spread the light and truth of Christ, so he tries to make us too busy to read our Bibles and pray and share the good news of the gospel. He tries to get us to fall into sin and move away from God. He lies to us and tells us God doesn't care about us. He discourages us when we are doing the Lord's work. He causes disunity in the church. He does whatever he can to stop us but we are the light! That light has the power of Christ and the devil can't defeat that unless we give up and let him. Let your light shine!

"Ye are the light of the world. A city that is set on an hill cannot be hid. Neither do men light a candle, and put it under a bushel, but on a candlestick; and it giveth light unto all that are in the house. Let your light so shine before men, that they may see your good works, and glorify your Father which is in heaven." ~Matthew 5:14-16.

Amazingly, just after I wrote that, the DJ on the radio said, "Let your light shine!" I love those little confirmations from the Lord! Hallelujah, God is so good!

Don't hide that light you have burning within you! Don't let our adversary, the devil, steer you away from shining. He most certainly will try, but we must put on the full armor of God to protect against his schemes and his lies.

Ephesians 6:14-17 says, "Stand therefore, having your loins girt about with truth, and having on the breastplate of righteousness; And your feet shod with the preparation of the gospel of peace; Above all, taking the shield of faith, wherewith ye shall be able to quench all the fiery darts of the wicked. And take the helmet of salvation, and the sword of the Spirit, which is the word of God."

This spiritual armor will preserve and protect you from the enemy in times of spiritual warfare. But if you back up a few verses to Ephesians 6:10, it states, *"Finally, my brethren, be strong in the Lord and in the power of his might."* Before you can have victory by putting on the full armor of God, you must be strong in the Lord and the power of His might. If your faith in God is weak, you will most certainly be ineffective in your spiritual battles. When David went up against Goliath, it was his faith in his big and mighty God that allowed him to kill the giant with just a sling and a stone. His faith in the Lord was strong and he knew that the power to defeat the enemy came from God.

If you are a Christian, the Lord will be continually testing and stretching your faith. He will allow you to be in situations where you will be in trouble if He doesn't come through for you. There will be absolutely nothing that you can do but trust in Him. It is very easy for us to say, "I trust You Jesus", but do we really trust Him? There have been times where I have thought that I had an unwavering trust in Him, but then something will be thrown at me that just totally shakes my faith and makes me realize that it's not as strong as I thought. It sends me to my knees, crying out to the mighty Jesus for help. When I finally come through the situation, my faith is strengthened a little more and I remember His goodness and mercy the next time I go through a time of testing. Remembering God's faithfulness to us in the past will help us to have faith for future trials. When you are struggling, you can pray, trust and remember how God has come through for you time and time again.

Chapter 19 - A Gently Beckoning Voice

In the past couple of weeks, I have been neglecting my writing due to all of the packing and moving to our new home. It has been quite a lot of work and has left me completely exhausted. I have still been making time to read God's Word and pray, but I really felt as though the Lord was calling me to continue my writing. It really is a wonderful thing, spending time with Him. The busyness has been taking me away from it for a time but I've been hearing the Holy Spirit calling me back to it. During all of the craziness of moving, I lost the charger to one of my electronic devices. I really wanted it back because that device was now dead. I prayed and searched, and prayed and searched some more. I was really and truly about to give up on looking for it because it was nowhere to be found. I thought that perhaps it had accidentally gotten thrown away while unpacking.

I finally decided to get my laptop out to begin writing again, and that was also dead since it was a few weeks since I had used it last. I had to go and get my power cord to be able to use it. Well, guess what I found? The charger I had been desperately searching for was wrapped up in my laptop computer cord! At

CHAPTER 19 - A GENTLY BECKONING VOICE

that moment, I truly felt that the Holy Spirit was saying to me, *"I've been waiting for you."* He waited for me to heed His gently beckoning voice to come back to my writing before giving me back what I was searching for.

I have discovered through my experience that if God wants us to do something, He will not be demanding about it (unless you are in immediate danger). He is a gentleman and will ask you to do what it is that He desires of you. He will give you gentle reminders and steer you in the right direction, but He is not harsh about it. However, if we decide not to do what the Lord asks of us, there may be consequences involved, depending on the situation. We may also miss out on a wonderful blessing. I strongly believe that it is always best to obey God's voice immediately, without hesitation. It will always result in the best possible outcome. When we delay and procrastinate or refuse to comply altogether, we are outside of God's will. That is not a safe place to be. I have stated this before, but it is so true: The safest place to be is within the will of God. That is why when the Lord asked me to write a book, I immediately told Him that I would do it. I told Him that I would not be able to do it without Him, but I was willing to do whatever He asked of me.

Whenever God makes a request of me now, I am reminded of the time that He told me to share my testimony with the church, which I shared in an earlier chapter. I delayed and procrastinated and did not obey for quite some time because I was afraid. I was quite stressed out and my spirit was not at peace until I did what the Lord asked me to do. I could have saved myself a lot of distress by acting immediately. Obedience is what He's looking for and you will not be at peace until you comply with what He tells you to do. That is something important to consider whenever the Lord makes a request of you.

"Therefore thou shalt love the Lord thy God, and keep his charge, and his statutes, and his judgments, and his commandments, alway."
~Deuteronomy 11:1

Chapter 20 - Peace in His Presence

I recall a time when I was standing on the fishing pier one morning about 4 years ago, praying and communing with the Lord. There was a mighty wind blowing, and leaves were flying around everywhere. In addition to that, the waves were crashing quite forcefully into the pier on which I was standing. It was quite a tumultuous scene. But in the midst of all that chaos, I felt so at peace in His presence. God reminded me that morning that no matter what is going on in my life, no matter what storms blow through, *no matter what,* I can find peace in His presence. He is my rock, my provider and my helper. He has never failed me and He never will. I had just come through a very difficult time in my life, but the Lord was there for me through every single minute of it. He carried me through it all. And here He was on that morning, reminding me of that.

That peace that the Lord gives us is something that is just inexplicable, and is often referred to as the peace that passes all understanding. If you have experienced it, then you know exactly what I am speaking of. The first time I experienced it was when I was a very new Christian. I recall I was sitting at my desk in my home office and was extremely upset about something. I was sobbing inconsolably. Suddenly, I just felt this unexplainable peace and calm just wash over my whole being. I stopped crying immediately and was quite amazed by it. That was the Comforter, the Holy Spirit, comforting me. I did not understand that at the time, however. I mentioned it to a Christian friend a couple of days later and she explained it to me. I believe that it is so important for a new Christian to have a mentor. It was a blessing to have someone to explain such things to me.

"And the peace of God, which passeth all understanding, shall keep your hearts and minds through Christ Jesus." ~Philippians 4:7

The presence and the peace of Christ is a treasure beyond anything this world could ever offer. Let us daily revel in that treasure. Put everything else aside, even if for just a few moments each day to just be still before the Lord. This treasure is there for the taking, but we must move forth and grab onto it and keep it. His peace and His presence are freely given to us, but so often we hold tightly to our worries and our anxieties and our stresses. It can be so difficult to let go of them though. We have to learn to unclasp our tightly balled up fists full of worries and lay them at the feet of Jesus, and receive with open hands and open hearts the peace that He wants for us. Breathe, let it all go, and receive His goodness.

"Peace I leave with you, my peace I give unto you: not as the world giveth, give I unto you. Let not your heart be troubled, neither let it be afraid." ~John 14:27

Let not our hearts be troubled or afraid, for that is what Jesus said. The Bible says, "Do not be afraid" many times. There are so many reminders from the Lord in His Word to live without fear and worry. God is well aware of our propensity for being stressed out and afraid, and that is why He tells us this so many times.

Live without fear of what tomorrow, or next week, or next month will bring. Our heavenly Father will take care of us no matter what comes our way. Our worrying will only steal our peace and our joy for today, and it will not change a thing. Worry gives nothing good, it only takes away.

Matthew 6:27 says, "Which of you by taking thought can add one cubit unto his stature?"

What the Lord is telling us here is that our stressing out about something will not change the situation. Give it to God and let Him take care of it. Life is so much sweeter when we trust in the Lord as our Provider. He is quite capable of making a way, even when it seems that there is no way. I have watched Him remove mountains in my life when things just seemed so impossible to me. What is impossible for man is never impossible for our all-powerful, all-knowing, all-seeing God. He already has our situations worked out before we even encounter them.

"And he said, The things which are impossible with men are possible with God." ~Luke 18:27

There is something amazing that happens when we fully put our trust in our Creator. Freedom happens. We discover that we have the freedom to live our lives in joy and peace, without all the stress and worry. We can rejoice, even in bad times, because we know our Savior is good and He cares about us. He is able to take our troubled waters and calm them in an instant. He can open doors that no one can shut. He can give us victory if we love, trust and obey Him.

If you are in step with what God's plan for your life is, He can use you greatly. Don't wander off the path that He has given you and get lost somewhere in the wilderness. We must do our best to avoid getting distracted and forget to follow where He is leading. That is one of Satan's tactics, distracting us. Our adversary will do his best to lead you off course by putting obstacles in your way and then make you think that there is a better way to go. Or he may just make you so busy doing other things that you neglect what God told you to do. I am dealing with that very thing right now. There are so many things distracting me from doing what I know that I should be doing, which is writing this book. We should follow the Lord wholeheartedly in faith and confidence, or we can end up wandering around in the desert for forty years as the Israelites did because of their disobedience and unbelief. I know that I do not want to be wandering. I want to stay on course and finish the race well.

"Brethren, I count not myself to have apprehended: but this one thing I do, forgetting those things which are behind, and reaching forth unto those things which are before, I press toward the mark for the prize of the high calling of God in Christ Jesus." ~ Philippians 3:13-14

Chapter 21 - Finding My War Room

We are all moved into our beautiful new home and are settling in nicely. We are very blessed to have a walk-in closet in our new home. It is so wonderful to have this room, not only as a space to put our clothing, but it is large enough to be a dressing room as well. It is probably the warmest room in the house, so it is such a blessing to be able to get dressed in there in the colder fall and winter months. I have discovered a third use for this wonderful little blessing of a room. I was feeling very cold the other night as I was heading for the closet to change for bed. My husband, who knew how cold I was feeling said to me, "Are you heading for the warm room?" I misheard what he said and thought that he said "war room". If you have seen the movie by that name, you know that one of the main characters turned her closet into a prayer closet. There is so much power in prayer, and in being a prayer warrior. God responds to it in a big and mighty way. Prayer is connecting with Him on an intimate level, and it allows us to come before His throne with thanksgiving for the many blessings that He bestows upon us. It also allows us to come to Him with our requests and with our distresses.

After that "war room" reference that I mistakenly heard from my husband, I started thinking that this would be an excellent place for a prayer closet. The thought has been with me since that evening, and just now I saw a verse of scripture from Matthew 6:6 which says, "But thou, when thou prayest, enter into thy closet, and when thou hast shut thy door, pray to thy Father which is in secret; and thy Father which seeth in secret shall reward thee openly." This has confirmed my thoughts about the prayer closet, and so I believe that God is in agreement with it. I have also, earlier this morning, signed up for a 31 day "pray for your marriage" challenge. This will be an excellent start to the challenge, to have a special place to go to pray fervently for my husband and my marriage each day. My plan is to pray first thing in the morning, before the busyness of the day takes over. I am taking this very seriously and I don't want anything to get in the way or make me forget. I know without a doubt that the enemy is going to do his best to distract me, but I refuse to let him. Each morning I will receive an email with a topic to pray for my husband about, such as his role as spiritual leader, his work, and his relationship with the Lord. God has already answered many prayers that I have prayed for my husband, so as a wife I truly should be praying for him every single day. He needs to be lifted up and covered in prayer as he goes out into the world each day and encounters many situations.

As I write this, it is a new day, and I did use the prayer closet this morning to start the prayer challenge and pray for my husband. It really was a special time spent with the Lord, and when I concluded my prayer for my spouse, the prayers just kept flowing out of me! There were so many people that I felt prompted to pray for so I just kept praying. I truly felt a connection with the Lord, just as I did when I used to go to the fishing pier to pray and commune with Him every day. I loved that place and I wish it was not so far from here because I truly miss my daily meetings with Jesus down at the river. It was such a special time for me and I pray that our meetings in the prayer closet will be just as special.

The following day, as I was in my prayer closet praying for my husband, I asked the Lord to send him a special blessing that day. I also asked Him to reveal Himself to my husband in some way on that day, so that Dale would experience His presence. A short while later I headed off to the grocery store to go shopping. As I was driving to the store, I suddenly felt that the Lord was telling me to stop at the local thrift store and look for a dollhouse for my granddaughters. They had recently been telling me that they wanted one and I really wanted to get it for them, but I knew that dollhouses can be quite pricey and I did not have the funds available to purchase such an expensive item. As I was driving, I started praying and I asked the Lord to please let me find what I was looking for if I was going to stop there. I don't ever recall seeing any dollhouses in that store, but since the Lord put it on my heart to stop there and look, I did. I went in and walked over to the toy section and found a lot of really neat toys there, as well as a very small dollhouse, but it was not what I was looking for. I was disappointed that I did not see one and was getting ready to leave when that "still, small voice" of God told me to go and look over by the furniture. I took a walk over to the section by the household furniture and I immediately saw a big, beautiful dollhouse sitting there, and it was even nicer than what I was looking for! It was probably about four feet high and had all the furniture and accessories with it. They must have just put it out because there was no price on it yet. I found a sales clerk and inquired about it, so she went and found a price for me. It was only $15, so I immediately told her I would take it.

It was quite a trick getting that large item in my trunk and tying it down, but I was determined and I got it done. It was so worth it to see how excited the girls were when they saw it! I felt as though this was as much of a gift from God's heart as it was mine, since He prompted me to stop at that thrift store and look for it just as they had most likely just put it out on the sales floor. I cried tears of joy because I had prayed that morning for the Lord to bless my husband and show Himself in some way to him, and for some reason God blessed *me* and showed Himself to *me*. I still tear up thinking about that.

I have come to discover that when I show up, the Lord shows up as well. When I intentionally come to meet with God in prayer and praise, He eagerly comes to that meeting. I feel as though He loves those meetings as much as I do. Jesus often withdrew to lonely places to pray, according to scripture. Even the Son of God went to be alone to pray to our Father in Heaven. He often sent the crowds away so that He could do so. He knew the importance of getting away from all of the clamor and commotion that surrounded Him to make time to be alone with God. If Jesus got away to pray, shouldn't we make it a point to pursue a quiet time of solitude with God each day as well? I believe quite strongly that Jesus was modeling the behavior which He wants from all of us, as He often did, many times in Scripture. Not only did He speak it, but He lived it. That is an important life choice that we, as Christians, can make daily to remain close to our Heavenly Father.

Chapter 22 - Exhibiting Holiness

We must be consistent in our walk with Christ. We should not go to church on Sunday morning and then live our lives as unholy heathens for the rest of the week. We must live godly lives every single day as an example for the rest of the world to witness the transforming power of Christ. We want to draw the lost world to Christ, not send them running away from Him because we aren't living like the "set apart" people of God that we should be. When we do not live godly lives, we can create a stumbling block for our brothers and sisters. As an example, you may believe that it is okay to go to a casino and gamble and drink alcohol. Your friend that sees that behavior may wish to do the same, thinking that if it is okay for a Christian to do it, then it must be okay for everyone. You may not have issues participating in those activities, but your friend may. They may become addicted to gambling or become an alcoholic. We must exhibit godliness to the best of our ability at all times and not create stumbling blocks for others. Live in a way that honors and glorifies God at all times. This especially applies to what we speak. From out of our mouths comes what is in our hearts, and it speaks volumes about us and what our beliefs are.

"Let no corrupt communication proceed out of your mouth, but that

CHAPTER 22 - EXHIBITING HOLINESS

which is good to the use of edifying, that it may minister grace unto the hearers." ~Ephesians 4:29

If we are speaking unholy things in the presence of others, they may question our faith. As Christians, we are representing Jesus Christ in all that we say and do. We must remember that and act accordingly. Our goal should be to draw in the lost, not drive them away with unholy behavior.

In modeling Christ-like behavior in our lives, we are showing the world what God has taught us through the reading of His Word in our Bibles and from listening to the leading of the Holy Spirit who indwells us when we are born again and saved. We also learn through going to church and hearing the Word of God preached, and by having godly relationships with other Christians. Many people have never read the Bible, and so they are witnessing it through us. How we act, speak and love others can make a huge impact on whether or not someone comes to know Christ. The world is watching, so let's make a positive impact!

Chapter 23 - Sharing the Gift of Jesus

It is currently the month of December and we are in the middle of a very joyous Christmas season in our new home. Our Christmas trees are lit up and brightly decorated with angels, snowmen, glass balls, bows, bells and stars. The inside and outside of our home is adorned with some very festive decorations and lights, and a beautiful nativity scene displayed on the hearth in front of the fireplace declares the reason for the season. Our gifts have been purchased and wrapped and will soon be placed under the tree. We are really enjoying this wonderful time of year and celebrating the birth of our Savior! The baking of cookies, pies and bread is also on our list of activities of the season. Christmas music fills the house with joyous songs about Jesus' birth. I have come to realize that although I have always loved listening to and singing Christmas carols since I was a child, I have only recently begun to know the true meaning of these songs. Before I accepted Christ as my Savior, they were just happy songs to sing during the Christmas season. I had no idea back then what I was really singing about. Now when I listen to the lyrics, I hear that they are filled with the salvation message and the true meaning of why Christ was born. He was born of a virgin in a stable in Bethlehem. He was fully God and fully man, at the same time. Jesus was born to

CHAPTER 23 - SHARING THE GIFT OF JESUS

die on a cross, to pay the debt for our sins so that we can have eternal life with Him in Heaven, if we accept Him as Lord and put our faith in Him.

What an amazing gift He has given us, the gift of salvation! His gifts don't stop there. He also offers us the gifts of true peace, true joy, and true love. These gifts are exclusively by Him and through Him. They cannot be fully and truly experienced without Jesus. He is freely handing these gifts to you, and all you have to do is reach out and accept them. They are yours to take, unwrap, keep and also to give away. The precious gift of salvation includes 3 things: forgiveness of our sins, eternal life in Heaven, and the ability to have a close personal relationship with the Lord. Peace, love and joy are added to that magnificent package to make it the perfect gift from Jesus to us. They are all paid for in full by our Savior. He paid that debt on the cross and now we have been set free from our bondage to sin. We are no longer captives enslaved to the enemy. We should now be lovers of righteousness and truth, serving the mighty Jesus and not the lowly Satan.

Let us take hold of those precious gifts being offered by the Lord and use them to further His mighty Kingdom. The most important way we can achieve this is by freely giving these gifts away to others and showing them and telling them about what the Lord Jesus has done for us. Share your testimony and how Jesus changed you. We should be ever faithful to fulfill the "great commission" in which Jesus commands,

"Go ye therefore, and teach all nations, baptizing them in the name of the Father, and of the Son, and of the Holy Ghost: Teaching them

to observe all things whatsoever I have commanded you: and, lo, I am with you alway, even unto the end of the world. Amen." (Matthew 28:19-20.)

Chapter 24 - Courage, Dear Heart

It is now the beginning of a new year and life is just moving along so quickly. Since it is a new year and a new beginning, I asked God for a new word for this year - a word that I can focus on and something that He wants me to work on. The word that He gave me is courage. Ironically, that word very much scared me at first. I started thinking about all the things that could be thrown my way to teach me courage. I had to stop myself and just remember what I already know - God is bigger than any situation that I may encounter, and there is nothing too hard for Him. He has shown me many times that I can trust Him in ALL things and that He is always with me.

"Have not I commanded thee? Be strong and of a good courage; be not afraid, neither be thou dismayed: for the Lord thy God is with thee whithersoever thou goest." ~Joshua 1:9

This verse was a promise from God to Joshua, as he was to lead the Israelites into the promised land after the death of Moses. They were God's words of encouragement to strengthen Joshua as he took on this tremendous new role. God gives us the same promise, to be with us always, in the Great Commission which is in Matthew 28:20. He also said in Hebrews 13:5, *"I will never leave thee, nor forsake thee."*

As long as I stay within God's will, I will have nothing to worry about. If I submit myself to Him at all times and remain faithful, humble and obedient, I will have nothing to fear. I can walk in confidence, knowing full well that I am covered by His grace. God is for me and He is on my side. As long as I keep that knowledge in my mind and in my heart, I can be at peace.

"The Lord is on my side; I will not fear: what can man do unto me?"
~Psalm 118:6

I have decided that I am going to embrace this word courage and I am excited to see what the Lord is going to do and show me this year!

I do know that the first thing that is going to take some courage is publishing this book. I am headed into uncharted territory for me. I do not have any experience with the whole book writing and publishing world and so I am praying for the Lord to lead me and guide me all the way through it. I know that since He has asked me to do this, He will be faithful to help me to get it done. I am solely relying on Him and Him alone in this whole process because I want this to be a testimony of what He can do through a nobody with a willing and surrendered heart. After the writing and publishing, the next challenge that will come for me is promoting it. I do not yet have any knowledge or experience with that aspect of the whole process, but I am trusting in the Lord to help me in a big and mighty way to get it done. I must remind myself often that where God guides, He provides.

CHAPTER 24 - COURAGE, DEAR HEART

"And the Lord shall guide thee continually, and satisfy thy soul in drought, and make fat thy bones: and thou shalt be like a watered garden, and like a spring of water, whose waters fail not." ~Isaiah 58:11

Chapter 25 - All for King Jesus

God is so good and I just want to give Him so much praise and glory for answered prayers. I am literally in awe of our great and mighty God. He answered not just one, but two of my prayers today. It never ceases to amaze and bless me how He provides without fail what I need when I ask Him. God is an amazing way maker and miracle worker and I am just so thankful to Him. Praise God from whom all blessings flow!

When God gives you an answer to your prayers or does something amazing in your life, by all means share it with people! It is quite evident to me that that is what God wants us to do. It is the reason why He told me to write this book. Non-believers as well as believers both need to hear these testimonies. Non-believers need to hear them because when they see what God has done in your life it just may draw them to the Lord, especially when they are going through a difficult time. They will see what the Lord has done for you and want the same in their own lives. This may result in the realization of their need for a Savior, and Jesus is the One that our hearts are all searching for. Believers also need to hear your testimonies because every person goes through trials and dark times in their lives. Your stories can bring them hope and renewed faith when they need it most. I love to hear other people's God stories because it just fills me with so much joy and awe to see the Lord at work in their lives. What an amazing thing it is to see what God is capable of doing.

When you are going through a trial in your life, come humbly before His throne and cry out to God for help with a pure and holy heart, and He will hear you and He will answer you in His perfect timing. Perhaps not exactly as you believe that He would or should, but just bear in mind that His way is the best way and His infinite wisdom is beyond our comprehension. He is not only working things out for your good, but also for a greater cause, which is His Kingdom.

All of the situations that we endure are in some way preparing us to be kingdom-minded disciples of Jesus. To be kingdom-minded is to center yourself under the Lordship of Jesus, and to focus your life on things of His Kingdom. In being kingdom-minded, you also choose to fulfill your God given purpose. That is the specific purpose that God has for you to further His Kingdom. Let me just explain a little bit about the Kingdom of God. The Kingdom, first and foremost, has a king - King Jesus. In order to enter His Kingdom, we are required to have a new birth. Our new birth is when we are saved, or born-again. This happens when we accept Jesus as our Lord and Savior and apply His death on the cross as payment for our sins. It also requires that we repent of our sin. When we have done that, we must then walk in our God-given purpose. When we walk in our purpose, we are taking part in the furthering of the Kingdom of God.

When you are obedient and submit yourself to His Lordship over you, He will work all things out for good. Not just some things, but ALL things, as it states very clearly in this passage in the Bible:

"And we know that all things work together for good to them that love God, to them who are the called according to his purpose." ~Romans 8:28

This applies to everything, including the bad things that others do to hurt you, the daily struggles, and that trouble that you got yourself into. So we can be confident that He will work it all out for our good and the good of His Kingdom, because His Word says so. God always does what He says He will do. Give it all to the Lord and seek Him with your whole heart, and then keep praying until you receive your answer.

There will be times where you will be just utterly amazed by what He will do. There will also be times when you will have to wait. While you are waiting, it is best to keep praising, worshiping, serving and obeying God. If you are in a time of waiting, straying from the Lord's commandments will put you at a great disadvantage. It will, in all likelihood, prolong your waiting. God will not hear you or bless you while you are disobeying Him.

A couple of nights ago, the Lord awoke me in the middle of the night and this is what I heard the Holy Spirit say to me - *"Obedience to God is the key to victory in the Christian life."* How true this is!

CHAPTER 25 - ALL FOR KING JESUS

"This book of the law shall not depart out of thy mouth; but thou shalt meditate therein day and night, that thou mayest observe to do according to all that is written therein: for then thou shalt make thy way prosperous, and then thou shalt have good success." ~Joshua 1:8.

This passage is saying that you will prosper spiritually if you meditate on and obey the words of God. Stay faithful to God in your waiting, and you will have victory in your spiritual life.

Leading victorious lives is what we all desire, isn't it? That victory starts with submitting to Jesus' lordship over us and continues on with obeying what He tells us. We must "die to self" each and every day and live for the King, the Lover of our souls, the One who died a gruesome death so that we could be forgiven and free. How could we do anything other than give Him our complete devotion, love and obedience? We should want to glorify Him every day in all of our actions, thoughts and words.

We must not let our failures in this area pull us further and further away from the Lord. We are all human and we are going to fail sometimes. We do not have to let those failures define us, however. If we catch ourselves doing something that we know we shouldn't be doing and we know is not pleasing to the Lord, we should immediately repent and go to Him in prayer and ask for forgiveness. "Dying to self" is denial of the flesh and it is a continual process of sanctification that we must choose each and every day. We are no longer living for ourselves and our own selfish desires. We now live for God's will and for His Kingdom.

"That ye put off concerning the former conversation the old man, which is corrupt according to the deceitful lusts; And be renewed in the spirit of your mind; And that ye put on the new man, which after God is created in righteousness and true holiness." ~Ephesians 4:22-24

We are now to put off our corrupt "old man", and put on our "new man". The "new man" is the spiritual man (or woman), and is righteous and holy.

In order to be in God's will, we have to give up our own will. When you become a born-again Christian, the Holy Spirit indwells us and slowly starts changing us into who we are in Christ. It is usually not an instantaneous thing, but happens over time. We must submit to Him daily and let Him lead us. We must learn to depend on Him for all things. We must also have the faith to realize that His way is sufficient, and not try to lean on our own strength and understanding.

Once you get in your mind that all situations and trials and blessings are all to change your character and make you more Christ-like, you will be at peace with the process. God wants us to draw near to Him always, in the good times and in the bad times. He wants a relationship with us that will endure all things. Pray when you are in a good place and at peace, and pray even more when you are struggling. Read and study your Bible often so that you can learn all you can about Him. When you are going through a difficult time, read it even more because He will speak to you through His Word. I have experienced this many times so I can tell you that it is absolutely true.

In my own observation, it truly seems that the most radically obedient lovers of Christ are those that He shows Himself to often and in a mighty way. The more you submit to Him, obey Him and seek Him, the more you will experience Him. This will open the door for Him to do supernatural things in your life. If you want more of Jesus, then chase after Him and keep on running after Him. Keep seeking Him with all of your heart. He will show up in amazing ways and you will be so blessed by His presence in your life.

"And ye shall seek me, and find me, when ye shall search for me with all your heart." ~Jeremiah 29:13.

Chapter 26 - Seeing the Good in the Struggle

There is currently a global pandemic that has been declared due to an outbreak of the COVID-19 Coronavirus. There is starting to be widespread panic due to this virus and many people are going out and clearing store shelves of basic necessities and food. The public schools are currently closed for an indefinite time; restaurants, bars, gyms and movie theaters are closed. Sports, concerts and other public events are also being canceled or postponed in an effort to slow down the spread of the virus. I honestly was not previously aware of how distressed people are over this situation because I don't watch TV. I have been paying close attention to it over the past few weeks and I can see why so many people are in a panic mode. Especially the elderly and those with underlying health problems that put them at greater risk of complications and death. This virus is wreaking havoc, and the whole world seems to be at a standstill because of it.

Our state and many others have "stay at home" orders at this time. Everyone must stay at home, with the exception of essential personnel such as medical workers, grocery workers, law enforcement, postal employees, etc. We are so grateful for their

CHAPTER 26 - SEEING THE GOOD IN THE STRUGGLE

dedication and service to us. We are only permitted to go out to get food and essentials, and also for doctor's appointments and things of that nature. Parents are homeschooling their children. Families are spending time together, perhaps growing closer and getting to really know each other and connect for the first time in a long while. In this age of technology, it's easy to lose that human connection with each other. Almost everyone is usually looking down at their phones, video games and other electronic devices seemingly lost in their own little world. Now I see families going for walks together and playing outside together. Everything has slowed down and suddenly our lives are not so rushed and busy. We have time to be a family again. We also have time to grow closer to God by prayer and meditation and through the reading of our Bibles.

As awful as this virus is and all the panic and worry that it is causing, there is some good that is taking place from the situation. All of our "idols" have been taken away such as sports, bars, casinos and shopping. Many people are also temporarily laid off from their jobs. These are just a few of the many idols that draw our attention away from our Creator. Now I am seeing a lot of people looking for hope and turning to God. It has been reported that Bible sales are way up and I've seen pictures of the Bible section in some stores being empty. The Lord uses these types of situations to get people to draw near to Him and cry out to Him for help in their desperate hour of need. I am praying for a mighty move of God and that we will experience a revival, the likes of which has not been seen in a very long while. I can envision it now – the church houses so full that many are outside peering in the windows, desperate to hear God's Word. Sound systems being broadcast out into the parking lots for the ones that couldn't get in. Preachers and the faithful out sharing the gospel on the streets, with many gathered around to hear it with hopeful and eager hearts. The joy that this thought elicits in me is immense and inexplicable. What a wonderful world it would be to have Jesus at the center of it all!

Since all the church buildings have been temporarily closed due to the social distancing mandates, many churches have taken to live streaming their services. The church that we attend is doing live streaming but is also doing drive-in style church on Sundays. We all stay in our parked cars in the parking lot while our beloved Pastor stands on a parade float platform to preach. We also have a small worship team leading us with music and singing. Our choir is not allowed to assemble due to the restrictions in place. We have a sound system broadcasting the sound into the parking lot. It is the next best thing to actually being in church with our brothers and sisters in Christ, but it will be such a sweet day when we can all be together again. Sometimes you just don't realize what you have until you don't have it anymore.

In all the madness that is occurring, I have a peace that passes all understanding. The Lord is my refuge and my strength. My peace comes from staying focused on Him and not on the storm. I wish that I could hug everyone that is worried and afraid and tell them about God's peace. This is not a surprise to God and He already has this all worked out. We can take comfort in the fact that He is always in control of every situation. Jesus offers us a supernatural peace when we trust in Him and come to Him and give Him our worries, anxiety and fears. With all that is

CHAPTER 26 - SEEING THE GOOD IN THE STRUGGLE

going with the pandemic, we all need Him desperately and we need the peace that He gives.

There are so many verses of Scripture in the Bible that speak of His peace. Here are just a few of them:

"And the peace of God, which passes all understanding, shall keep your hearts and minds through Christ Jesus." ~Philippians 4:7.

"Peace I leave with you, my peace I give unto you: not as the world giveth, give I unto you. Let not your heart be troubled, neither let it be afraid." ~John 14:27.

"Thou wilt keep him in perfect peace, whose mind is stayed on thee: because he trusteth in thee." ~Isaiah 26:3.

Jesus loves us so much and He does not want us to worry and be afraid. He has gotten us through every trial thus far, and He will get us through this one as well.

This morning I was praying about being able to get the things that we need while things are so crazy. Due to the pandemic, my husband and so many others are not currently working. The store shelves are empty and it is difficult to impossible to get certain items, such as paper products, cleaning supplies, meats and many other food staples. I really felt that the Lord told me this morning, "I will provide". A little while later as I was praying again, the Lord reminded me about the fact that one of the names of God is Jehovah Jireh, which means "the Lord will provide". Amazingly, just after I got done praying, I saw a prayer that someone had just posted on social media that said,

"Dear Lord, You are Jehovah Jireh, the Lord who provides". I'm totally blown away every time the Lord tells me something like that and then soon after gives me a confirmation about what He said. He literally answered my prayer and then confirmed what He said. How awesome and amazing is that? Needless to say, I am not going to worry about not being able to get the things that we need because God told me He will provide. He is always faithful to do what He says. He has never failed me, and He never will. I can't say this enough: God is so good!

We all go through fiery trials in our lives. As I have previously said, God uses these trials to help us grow spiritually. But this time is quite different – The whole world is going through this particular trial at the same time. Since this is affecting every one of us in one way or another, I feel quite certain that God is and will be moving in a big and mighty way. He is going to use this devastating situation for the good of His Kingdom and for the good of His children. We've been shaken from our comfortable little lives and thrown into the fiery furnace. But just as in Daniel chapter 3, when Shadrach, Meshach and Abednego were thrown into the fiery furnace by King Nebuchadnezzar, Jesus is in the furnace with His faithful ones.

This morning I woke up thinking about how at the beginning of the year I asked the Lord for a focus word for the year, and the word that kept coming to my mind was "courage". I recall being somewhat distressed at this word as I started imagining all of the situations that I could encounter that would teach me courage. I had no idea at that time that we would very shortly be facing a worldwide pandemic. I didn't know that I would have to summon every ounce of courage in me to face

CHAPTER 26 - SEEING THE GOOD IN THE STRUGGLE

it without fear. I didn't know that my husband and so many others would be temporarily laid off from their jobs. I didn't know how disconcerting it would be to go into a grocery store, with every person wearing masks and gloves and having to keep my distance from everyone. I didn't know I'd be listening to the news reports of all the people dying alone with no family permitted to be with them, and how there were things like "temporary morgues" set up in refrigerated trucks in New York. I didn't know that I wouldn't be able to see my family and my grandchildren, and that I'd miss them like crazy because we'd have to stay away from each other to avoid contracting and spreading the virus.

So, courage was absolutely the most appropriate word for this year. Not just for me, but for all of us. My courage is coming from my faith in the Lord and His promises. I have faith that He is going to take care of us. I have faith that He will provide. I have faith that He is there to comfort us in our time of distress. I have faith that when I die, I will go to Heaven because my faith is in Jesus and His sacrifice on the cross. But the thing that I was reminded of this morning was the fact that Jesus also knew fear. When He was in the Garden of Gethsemane praying to God, He knew what was coming. He knew that He would be arrested, beaten beyond recognition and nailed to a cross and crucified. He was in such distress that He was literally sweating drops of blood. His prayer to God the Father was, *"O my Father, if it be possible, let this cup pass from me: nevertheless not as I will, but as thou wilt."* He was afraid, but He loves us so much that He was willing to endure the cross for us, to pay the penalty for our sin so that we can be forgiven and free. Facing the cross undoubtedly took a great deal of courage. I just cannot even fathom how Jesus was feeling through all of that. Even though His death was horrific, it was done for the good of mankind. Just as even though the current pandemic is awful, there will be some good that will come of it.

If you are not yet a born-again believer in Jesus Christ, now is the time to put your trust in Him and how His death, burial and resurrection conquered sin, death and Hell, and receive His peace, love and joy. You will be so glad that you did and you will never regret it. Your eternal destiny depends on it. God does not want to send people to Hell. People who reject God send themselves there. We all have a choice to make and we have the ability to choose Heaven (eternal life) or Hell (eternal punishment). If you don't choose God, you are choosing Hell. If you choose to repent of your sin and believe on the Lord Jesus Christ, you will have eternal life in Heaven with Him when you die. That is the truth that is in God's Holy Word, the Bible. You can experience for yourself the goodness and mercy of God. You can claim His all consuming love and His perfect peace for your own. He will forgive your sins, heal your brokenness and make you new. What can this world possibly offer that is better than that?

About the Author

Darlene Gail Wells was raised in Deer Park, New York and she currently lives in Fair Hill, Maryland with her husband Dale. She enjoys gardening, nature photography, bird watching, going hiking with her husband, and spending time with her children and grandchildren. What truly brings joy to her soul is worshiping Jesus. She became a born again Christian on April 15, 2011.

If you would like to watch live-streamed and previously recorded sermons from our Pastors at Pleasant View Baptist Church, the website address is: https://www.pvbchurch.com

You can connect with me on:
- http://darlenegailwells.website2.me
- https://twitter.com/JesusGrlDarlene
- https://www.facebook.com/LettingGodReign
- https://www.pvbchurch.com

www.ingramcontent.com/pod-product-compliance
Lightning Source LLC
Chambersburg PA
CBHW031448040426
42444CB00007B/1019